THE ESSENCE
OF SELF-DEFENSE

HIDY OCHIAI

Contemporary Books, Inc.
Chicago

Library of Congress Cataloging in Publication Data

Ochiai, Hidy.
    The essence of self-defense.

    Includes index.
    1. Self-defense.   2. Exercise.   I. Title.
GV1111.025   613.7'1   78-24186
ISBN 0-8092-7378-0
ISBN 0-8092-7377-2 pbk.

Published simultaneously in Canada by
Beaverbooks, Ltd.
150 Lesmill Road
Don Mills, Ontario M3B 2T5
Canada

Published by Contemporary Books, Inc.
180 North Michigan Avenue, Chicago, Illinois 60601
Manufactured in the United States of America
Library of Congress Catalog Card Number: 78-24186
International Standard Book Number: 0-8092-7378-0 (cloth)
                                    0-8092-7377-2 (paper)

Published simultaneously in Canada by
Beaverbooks
953 Dillingham Road
Pickering, Ontario L1W 1Z7
Canada

Contents

Preface

Throughout the United States today, self-defense instruction of one kind or another is being offered more and more at such places as YMCAs, YWCAs, boys' clubs, girls' clubs, and "continuing education" courses for adults at colleges and universities. And karate and judo and other forms of self-defense are now commonly accepted as academically accredited courses in the regular physical education curricula of the nation's high schools, colleges, and universities. This support of, and enthusiasm for, self-defense instruction outside the professional martial arts schools is a logical response by the general public—especially those citizens without access to such schools—to the ever-increasing number of violent crimes in our neighborhoods and on our streets. Citizens are aware that self-defense techniques may be crucial in an emergency, and thus they take their first steps along the path of basic martial arts instruction.

Now it goes without saying that one cannot expect to become invincible in self-defense situations after taking ten lessons in two months, but there are definite benefits to be obtained from a short course in karate or self-defense, not the least of which is the realization of the absurdity of violent behavior in a civilized society. Students of self-defense learn that one can detest violent behavior without having to fear it. Because of this, the benefits of self-defense training transcend the physical benefits (substantial as these are). The students also develop attitudes of increased self-confidence and an appreciation of the concept of inner peace.

Probably the best way to obtain the benefits of self-defense instruction is through formalized training in the traditional martial arts, such as karate, judo, or kendo—but these are not easy to learn in a very short time. To become proficient in any of the traditional martial arts you would need to demonstrate tremendous dedication and effort under an authentic teacher for a long period. Even though you may be willing to do this, such a program may not be available to you. (If the nearest professional martial arts school is over a hundred miles away, it would probably be unrealistic for you to attend regularly.) This book is intended to help those persons who wish to study self-defense but do not have the proper opportunity elsewhere. If that applies to you, then this book is written for you.

Of course, this book is also designed to be a suitable text for classroom (or gymnasium) instruction in the art of self-defense. If possible, a student should take instruction under a qualified teacher in order to more fully understand and digest the explanations in the text. The basic self-defense techniques presented here are not overly complicated, but they can be quite difficult to master, depending on the level of proficiency you wish to pursue. However, these basic techniques are more easily digested and understood than the broad range of physical and mental concepts involved in the eformal study of the traditional martial arts.

Since my primary intention is to make the text easily approached and understood by those with no previous martial arts training, I have deliberately avoided making it too technical. Many of the self-defense techniques must be explained in the terms of basic karate or other martial arts in order to teach them in an orderly and effective manner; so, when formal karate techniques are needed, they are explained and taught in this book. However, to prevent possible confusion, I have not used any of the technical terms from the original language of karate; all terms are translated into English.

Although the techniques covered are fundamental ones, they have numerous *applications*. If you are fortunate enough to have a qualified instructor, he or she will provide you with, and help you to find, many possibilities for applying these techniques. In the case of self-study, you can still discover various applications once you truly understand and practice the lessons. I cannot emphasize enough that *you can successfully self-study these techniques if you have the proper attitude of determination and discipline.*

This book is purposely divided into twelve lessons. Many so-called minicourses in self-defense are offered in one-, two-, or three-month

units, with the students meeting once or twice per week for four-, eight-, or twelve-week periods. In such cases, the instructor should adjust the scope of each lesson as needed, or cover only a portion of the lesson in class and have the students cover the remaining portions on their own. The division of the text makes such adjustments very easy to design.

If you are about to study these lessons on your own, you are strongly advised to follow them step by step because the lessons are, in most cases, progressive in nature. You may spend one hour or one week on each lesson; then, when you have gone through the entire book you might come back to the first lesson and review all the lessons. You might choose to spend a lot of time mastering each individual technique before going on to the next one.

I should also mention that although I used a partner (or "opponent") in order to demonstrate various techniques, it is not absolutely necessary that you have a partner when you study these lessons. When you practice alone, it is important to use the concept of the "imaginary opponent." Whatever method you use in your efforts to master the material will require willpower and determination to produce a positive result. The old cliché still applies: "Where there's a will, there's a way."

In its most desirable form, the art of self-defense includes the mental aspects of self defense, as well as the practical techniques. Try to give equal balance to both aspects of your training. This book also teaches you breathing exercises, an essential element in learning mental and physical control, and (eventually) harmony of mind and body. Without knowledge and practice of the proper breathing method, you may not be able to maximize the effectiveness of your physical strength and your mental power if you are forced to defend yourself.

Because the essence of self-defense includes important elements of physical fitness and body conditioning, this book begins with the basic physical exercises. It is extremely important to remember that each individual should engage in body conditioning exercises *according to his or her pace and level*. It goes without saying that these exercises can be modified according to an individual's need and physical capability. Your practice session, whether you are alone or in a group, must start with many of these warm-up exercises; at the end of the session, you should perform them with somewhat less intensity.

You may ask why the essence of self-defense should include such an emphasis on physical fitness. It must be obvious that you can execute acquired physical techniques more effectively if you are in good physical condition than if you are not. And do not forget that physical fitness is directly related to mental health. Surely you have had the experience of feeling better emotionally when you were in proper physical condition than when you were not. It follows that you might run less risk of getting into a hostile situation requiring self-defense if you are in good physical *and* mental condition. Your general alertness and patience will improve hand in hand as you practice body conditioning exercises. Thus, if you *do* meet with a situation requiring the application of self-defense techniques, you should be able to utilize your physical strength and mental concentration in a more effective manner if they are both strong and stable. In addition, the most basic reason for the direct relationship between physical fitness and self-defense may be that the essence of self-defense has to be seen as *a program of total self-development* for each individual, and to pretend that physical fitness is not an important part of self-development is surely a mistake.

Whether you practice alone or in a group, adhere strictly to the following rules:

1. Always keep yourself clean and sanitary, especially when practicing in a group.

2. Cut your fingernails and toenails regularly. (Again, especially in group practice so that you do not hurt yourself or others. Nails can tear the skin easily.)

3. Avoid both a full stomach and a completely empty stomach before practice. Very light food, such as juice and toast, should be sufficient about thirty to forty-five minutes before a full workout.

4. When you practice with a partner, you must concentrate 100 percent on executing your techniques *with control.* There is no reason why practice in the art of self-defense has to be dangerous. You and your partner must trust each other to control techniques and respect each other's safety.

5. The essence of self-defense includes the development of concentration and self-discipline so that you can apply these mental qualities to other areas of your practical daily living, whether at work, in school, or at home with your family. Therefore, you must make a conscious effort to develop your ability to concentrate and relax, and to practice the concept of self-discipline in action.

6. In group practice, no matter how informal it may be, you must show appropriate respect to your instructor and your fellow students. Of course, this attitude of respect must be spontaneous and sincere rather than artificial and awkward.

7. In group practice, do not compete against others in terms of progress. Rather, compete against yourself. The emphasis should be placed on the development of your own mental and physical improvement in relationship to your own potential.

8. Remember that you will gain as much as you put forth. If you are to follow this book on your own, it is imperative that you practice regularly and patiently.

9. For your practice, all you need to wear are a pair of loose pants and a loose shirt (such as sweat pants and a sweat shirt). In addition, in a self-study situation it will be particularly helpful if you can find a full-length mirror to correct your posture and technique (though this is not a must).

10. And most important, review each lesson before you go on to the next one.

11. Finally, please remember that there is no special "easy" way to the attainment of techniques in the art of self-defense, although there is certainly a "correct" way. Consistent step-by-step practice in accordance with this book's contents is the shortest and most effective way to the true proficiency you seek in the art of self-defense.

Introduction

Self-defense is defending oneself against acts of physical aggression and violence that endanger you and/or your loved ones. In order to achieve effective self-defensive action, you must attain and maintain a certain level of proficiency in the art of self-defense itself. At the same time, you must understand that self-defense involves "mental strength" as much as physical capability.

To defend yourself without giving your opponent an injury—or giving your opponent only a minimal injury—you must achieve a higher level of proficiency than that alluded to above. Although cases may occur in which you cannot think of the opponent's safety because you are overwhelmed by his attack, there are also cases in which you can reflect on the situation and take care of it with the minimum use of "violent" physical action. For example, it is not necessary to attack your opponent's eyes with your fingers if you can deal with the situation by simply throwing him to the ground or by delivering an effective punch to his ribs. Of course, if you are absolutely forced to go all the way—as in a situation that almost requires you to choose between your life and your assailant's life—you must defend yourself with every means possible.

Ostensibly, the art of self-defense is not difficult, but its seeming simplicity is deceiving. The complications and challenges increase for those who really wish to pursue them and to become truly proficient. Self-defense involves much more than just blocking, dodging, kicking, punching, and throwing. Even plain blocking and dodging are not easy to execute in "natural" situations, for there are numerous varieties of such situations that you must consider. "Practice makes perfect," the old cliché, accurately describes proper training in the art of self-defense.

Even if you do learn sufficient variations of self-defense techniques, and even if a certain situation with which you are familiar does occur, this does not mean that you can use the technique immediately and effectively to defend yourself. It is one thing to be able to block and throw your partner in the classroom, and it is quite another thing to be able to block and throw an actual assailant on the street.

The true difficulty, then, in asserting the value of learning self-defense techniques in a short course is based on the following points: (1) Such a course cannot cover all of the possible self-defense situational techniques, for these techniques are almost infinite in their forms and varieties; (2) in an actual situation, your mind will probably react differently than it does in the classroom.

This actually happened at midnight on a street in a large city: a rather skillful karate student was attacked by a mugger, but was unable to protect himself because he "froze." Of course, this particular incident should not encourage anyone to discredit the art of karate itself for being ineffective, for this karate student obviously did not represent the art adequately. This example merely illustrates how important it is to train your mind as well as your physical techniques and your strength. It must be remembered that your physical skills are nothing unless they are used properly and effectively, and only your mind will make that possible.

Let us re-emphasize one of the above points: it is extremely important to acknowledge that no matter how many situational techniques you learn and practice, *they will never cover all of the possible situations that might occur on the streets or anywhere else,* for the forms and variations of actual self-defense situations may be almost infinite in number.

This does not mean, however, that the importantance and value of study and practice are negated. Proper training provides first of all an opportunity to develop physical fitness, coordination, agility, and (through constant practice and effort) timing and balance—all of which you can eventually apply in executing self-defense techniques.

In addition to improving your physical qualities (and thus imparting all the benefits that accompany such improvements), learning various situational prearranged techniques will help you develop more self-confidence as you expand your awareness of the potential range of your physical strength and control. This confidence, one of the most important mental qualities, will make it possible for you to avoid places and situations where you are most likely to become imvolved in danger and violence. True confidence, which shines from within, makes you calmer and more peaceful, and consequently less belligerent. It is a fact that a well-trained person who is confident that he can take care of himself in a self-defensive predicament, can walk away from trouble without fear or panic.

Because perfection (or at least the attainment of proficiency) in any art or sport requires perseverance and constant effort, you will naturally acquire *the mental strength of self-discipline* if you are sincere and serious in pursuing this course of study. This, in turn, produces patience and self-respect, as well as respect for others. As you practice more and more, you will definitely acquire better mental control and greater physical well-being. These gains will enable you to better accomplish your work, your academic tasks, your familial duties, and so on. (This alone should make it worthwhile to study the art of self-defense and discover its true essence.)

I personally hope and pray that someday our society becomes such that we do not have to study self-defense techniques for practical purposes, but only for the sake of the art and for physical fitness. Unfortunately, however, the reality is that our everyday life is threatened by ever-increasing violence, so that although decent and law-abiding persons never look for trouble, they had better be able to defend themselves. It should go without saying that we must obey and respect law enforcement officials whenever they are carrying out their public duties in dealing with crimes and dangerous situations. Even in your own self-defense situations, if law enforcement officials are available in time, it is best to leave the situation to them. So when we talk about self-defense situations in this book, we are referring to such situations as your being choked by an assailant or your being attacked by a mugger—in other words, to situations in which you have no other recourse but your own self-defensive ability.

This book presents many situational self-defense techniques in condensed and formalized patterns that can be practiced easily by a single person or a group. One might argue that these formalized patterns are worthless because a mugger on the streets will not attack in the way that you want him or her to or in the way that you "assume" he or she will. This argument is valid up to a certain point; indeed, you cannot expect your "real" situations to occur in an expected, formalized pattern. However, you must keep in mind that these prearranged techniques for practice represent the "grammar" of self-defense. Without knowing any grammar, it is hard to learn languages. Of course, the important thing is to learn how to apply these grammatical forms. It is a fact that many Japanese high school and college students are excellent in English grammar but that the majority of them do not understand how to communicate well through spoken English. However, grammars should not remain mere grammars. They must be applied and made "alive." Likewise the "grammar" of self-defense techniques must be brought to life through constant practice according to the correct ways and methods. It is neither practical nor wise to *seek* opportunities for applying the grammar of self-defense on the streets in *actual* situations. But by a certain mental attitude during your practice, you can certainly seek progress and eventual proficiency. In other words, when you practice, *imagine* that you are actually engaged in a self-defense situation. Make your practice a mental exercise as well as a physical one.

One important thing that will undoubtedly help you to increase your mental strength and bring you into a proper "atmosphere" for self-defense practice is "ki-a-i." Ki-a-i is often explained as merely "shouting" or "yelling" in order to produce more effective and stronger power from the body. This is not entirely correct, for when you are at an advanced level you can execute a good ki-a-i without obvious shouting or yelling.

The *ki* of ki-a-i is a Japanese word that describes such things as spirit, mind, heart, mood, care, air, and atmosphere, but above all, in terms of the martial arts, it connotes a certain invisible quality that bridges and harmonizes mind and body. The *a-i* of ki-a-i denotes the meeting and coordinating of the timing and focus of the techniques of the martial arts at the moment of their execution.

Ki-a-i may be defined, therefore, as that which makes it possible to maximize the effectiveness of those techniques by coordinating and concentrating physical and mental strength through the proper exhalation of air from the lower abdomen. It is true that ki-a-i is usually accompanied by a loud and strong shouting or yelling, but mere shouting does not mean a good ki-a-i, and a good ki-a-i may or may not produce a loud shouting or yelling. In the practice of ki-a-i, it is best to use the sounds "taa-a," "saa-a," and /or "yaa-a."

Ki-a-i is a must if a technique is to be strong and effective. It should also be remembered that a technique without "focus" is meaningless, for it is like an arrow without a proper target. Ki-a-i makes it possible to execute a technique with focus, because it increases your ability to concentrate. Executing a technique with ki-a-i is like utilizing all of the available weapons in order to attack the enemy—without thinking that you will get a second chance. In this way the muscles and nerves of your body will be concentrated at the moment of focus. This is the meaning of ki-a-i.

As has already been implied, ki-a-i is not a method of uttering a word. It is a method of breathing. By means of proper inhalation and exhalation through the abdominal region, you properly coordinate the muscles and the nerves of the body. As for the breathing method itself, please refer to Chapter 1H. Theoretically, ki-a-i can be divided into four categories: ki-a-i with sound; ki-a-i without actual, obvious sound; short ki-a-i; and long ki-a-i.

The distinction between sounded and unsounded ki-a-i is not overly significant as long as the ki-a-i is executed properly through the power that emanates from the lower abdominal region. However, it is easier (and quite effective) to accompany your ki-a-i with a large and strong sound. In self-defense situations, your loud ki-a-i might even scare your opponent and thus increase your courage to do whatever you feel you must do.

The most powerful kind of ki-a-i is the shortest one. This is delivered simultaneously with a strong exhalation of air through the mouth. The short ki-a-i must be executed at the exact moment of punching, kicking, or striking, just as fire is made only when two stones are struck against each other in an instantaneous strong strike. You may use the long and loud ki-a-i before your actual execution of a technique. When two fighters meet in a formal combat, each might use the long ki-a-i before the two actually exchange the techniques. The long ki-a-i encourages each fighter, and each may try to intimidate the other with it.

It is difficult to generalize, but you may safely say that in delivering an *attacking* (offensive) technique, especially when you intend it to be the final technique, you may use a short and strong ki-a-i with a loud sound or shouting voice, whereas in *blocking* your opponent's attack, you may use a short and strong ki-a-i without a loud sound. A long and loud ki-a-i may be effective in a situation in which you utilize a submission technique. In any case, you may use all kinds of ki-a-i and find out what is best for you in each situation.

In conclusion, ki-a-i gives a certain force—spiritual, physical, and mental—which makes it possible for us to move our bodies in a more coordinated way. The muscles and nerves of the body move more effectively and smoothly through the proper use of ki-a-i. Needless to say, ki-a-i alone is not enough for self-defense. It is important that you do not neglect the values of physical techniques, especially basic ones. Even if you can execute a good ki-a-i, if your techniques are not correctly polished, your effort will be in vain. That is why you must try to learn and practice each basic technique patiently until you can perform it spontaneously. Practice each technique slowly, step by step, in the beginning, and then gradually increase your speed and power in performing it. When you feel that you have been successful in familiarizing yourself with a technique, start to execute it with a good ki-a-i and with the feeling that you are engaged in an actual self-defense situation.

1

Physical conditioning exercises

In order to become fairly proficient in the art of self-defense it is not necessary to be super-strong physically. In other words, you don't have to be like a professional athlete. However, in order to make your self-defense techniques most effective once you are forced to defend yourself, it is desirable to be physically fit; so, according to your own pace and physical capability, you should try to make yourself more coordinated, stronger, more agile, faster, and so on (not as compared with others but in relationship to your own potential). Of course, this is not only for the sake of practical self-defense techniques; it also feels better if you are in proper physical condition. After all, the essence of self-defense includes an individual's total welfare in daily living, and if you are physically fit and mentally stable, the chances are that you can cope better with various situations in life. Self-defense, therefore, in the most profound sense of the word, includes overcoming obstacles and difficulties in life through a self-disciplined mind.

Described below are various exercises that will increase your agility, strength, coordination, stamina, and overall power if you diligently perform them every day. What you must keep in mind constantly is the basic rule that you perform each exercise according to your own physical capability and stamina. Each individual has a different pace, and he or she should keep it always.

A. Running and/or walking in place. To start with, it is good to run in place or just walk in place for the sake of generally loosening up the whole body.

B. Half knee bends. This exercise is primarily a transitional one. In other words, it is effective to do this particular exercise between running and, say, push-ups. The half knee bends exercise gives your heart a chance to rest, and it also tones the muscles and improves blood circulation.

1. Stand straight with the shoulders relaxed. (Keep your back straight, since this exercise is also effective in developing a good posture.)

2. Bring both arms up and forward.

3. Bring the arms down and stand on the balls of the feet, bending the knees.

4. Still standing on the balls of the feet, straighten the knees and bring the arms straight forward again. After this, as you come down on the heels, drop the arms down. Repeat the whole procedure four to five times.

Let's look at this exercise from a side view.

5.

6.

7.

8.

C. Side swings. Relax your shoulders and arms, and swing the upper body lightly, together with the arms and the neck. In the beginning, twist your body only halfway, but gradually try to look directly behind yourself.

1.

2.

1. Stand straight, with feet apart and shoulders relaxed.

2. Turn neck to right (slightly).

D. Loosening the neck. Turn the neck from right to left, and up and down. Again, it's important that you keep your shoulders relaxed and your eyes open as you move your head.

3. Turn neck to left (slightly).

4. Turn neck up.

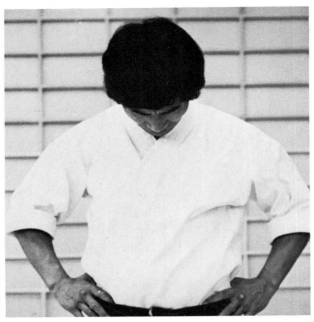

5. Turn neck down.

6. For additional loosening, you may wish to rotate the neck clockwise and counterclockwise.

7.

8.

1. Stretch slightly to side.

2.

E. Light stretching. This exercise, like many others, should be practiced according to each individual's pace and physical capability. Those who are not accustomed to this type of exercise should be very careful not to overstretch or hurt the muscles. It should be kept in mind that you develop your strength and agility gradually, and not overnight.

3. Stretch slightly to side on ball of foot

4.

5. Stretch deeply on heels.

6.

F. Intensive stretching. As stated earlier, stretching exercises must be done carefully, according to individual physical capability. However, if your physical capability allows, the following pictures can be your guide for intensive stretching.

1.

2.

3.

4.

5.

6. In group practice, your partner can push gently forward and sideward as shown.

7.

8.

G. Push-ups. There are several kinds of push-ups, as shown in the photos below. The most common one is done with both hands open, palms flat on the floor. This push-up helps mainly to strengthen the arms and the shoulders, as well as improve the general tone of the upper body. Knuckle push-ups are used mainly to build up the arm and shoulder muscles. It is suggested that you begin with the normal flat-hands push-ups. Later, if you desire to build up the arm and shoulder muscles, you may begin the knuckle push-ups.

1. Normal flat-hands push-ups.

2.

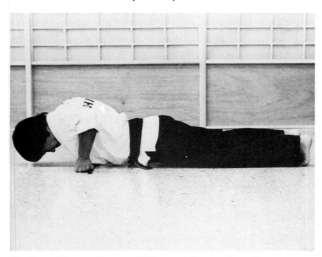

3. Knuckle push-ups (side and front views)

4.

5.

6.

7. Three-finger push-ups (side and front views).

8.

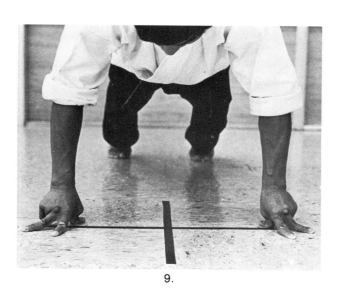

9.

10.

11. Back-wrist push-ups. These are not mandatory. They are for persons who would like a more difficult exercise that is specifically intended for wrist development.

12.

13.

14.

15. One-arm push-ups. Again, this is not for the average self-defense student.

16.

17. Knee push-ups. If you find normal push-ups too strenuous, it is suggested that you start with knee push-ups.

18.

H. Deep abdominal breathing. After the push-ups, it is important to take three or four deep breaths before going on to the next exercises. The following is a brief explanation of the method by which you are advised to perform the deep abdominal breathing exercise.

1. Start to breathe in through the nose as if you were trying to find the "smell" or "taste" of the air.
2. Keep the shoulders relaxed, and as you keep inhaling through the nose, try to push your diaphragm downward, thus pushing your stomach outward.
3. After inhalation is completed, open your mouth and start to exhale through it. The process should be gradual. As you exhale, push your diaphragm upward and your stomach in.

4. As you see in photo 2, during the exhalation stage you take a stance with both knees bent inward. Both hands start out from the sides of your hip, and as you exhale, you push the hands down and out with the feeling of squeezing the air out from the bottom of your stomach. For the breathing-out motion, just bend your knees inward slightly as you point both feet inward.

1. Inhale through nose, and send air to lower abdomen.

2. As you exhale, turn knees inward.

3. Complete exhalation of air.

Again, breathing exercises must be performed according to your individual capabilities. *More harm than good can result if you abuse an exercise by trying to do more with it than your body is ready for.*

I. Loosening the wrists and ankles. Shake your wrists up and down and side to side. Turn your ankles in both directions to loosen them, and also move your toes to improve blood circulation and toning.

1.

2.

3.

4.

5.

6.

7.

8.

J. Sit-ups. If a partner is available, you may have your partner hold both of your feet while you perform sit-ups.

1. Regular sit-ups.

2.

3. Sit-ups with knees bent. (Same benefits as regular sit-ups.)

4.

5. Sit-ups with partner.

6.

7.

8.

K. Turning the upper body. Turn your whole upper body in both directions, together with your arms. The feet should be 1½ shoulder widths apart.

1.

2.

3.

4.

L. The windmill body twist. Twist your body downward, and touch your fingers to your feet. Hold this position for eight to ten seconds.

1.

2.

M. Lifting partner on back. This exercise is, of
course, possible only if you have a partner.
It stretches your back, and at the same time
it strengthens your legs and knees.

1.

2. The person being lifted should remain **completely**
relaxed.

3. If you are in good physical condition and wish to
strengthen your legs and hips, you may bend your
knees up and down as you lift.

1. Bend forward slightly, with the feet widely apart.

2. Bend forward deeply.

N. Bending the body forward and backward. Widen your stance, and bend your upper body forward and backward as much as you can.

3. Bend backward slightly.

4. Bend backward deeply.

1.

2. Rotate to the right, then to the left.

O. Turning the knees. Relax both knees and pivot them lightly, with the feet kept together.

3.

4.

P. Swinging and pulling the arms

1.

2.

3.

4.

Q. Loosening the thighs and ankles
  1. Hold feet tightly.
  2. Flex thighs downward.
  3. From the standing position it is difficult to loosen the ankles. Here is an easier way. Continue as shown in photo 4.

1.

2.

3.

4.

R. The relaxation posture. After you have completed the exercises explained above, *but* before you continue to the actual practice of the self-defense techniques, it is meaningful to take the so-called relaxation posture for about thirty seconds to one minute.

1. Lie down on your back as shown in the photo, and relax completely.
2. Close your eyes lightly, and try to get rid of all your self-consciousness.
3. Try to relax the entire body, beginning with the fingers, the toes, and the shoulders.
4. Consciously try to detach yourself from everything for a moment.
5. Concentrate on the rhythm of your breathing, which should be quiet and slow.
6. *Count* every time when you breathe out.

This particular posture is not only beneficial in terms of physical relaxation, but most important, it is directly related to your mental and emotional relaxation as well. Because of this special posture-exercise, you can concentrate better and more deeply on whatever you are supposed to do.

S. Extra calisthenics. For those who find the preceding exercises insufficient, here are some that are a little more involved.

1. Jumping high with (*a*) knees bent and (*b*) knees straight.

a.

b.

2. Standing on toes.

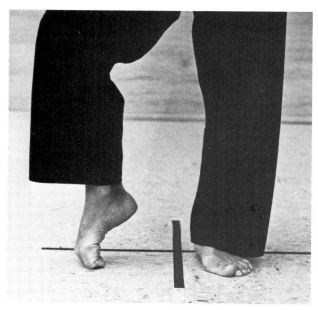

a. One foot on toes.

b. Both feet on toes.

3. Full squat and front kick. In performing the
full squat, keep feet flat on floor.

a.

b.

c.

d

4. High knee kick.

a.

b.

5. Stretching with a bar or a ladder.

a. With toes straight up.

b. With toes to the side.

6. Stretching back on the knees. (This exercise is sometimes dangerous for those with knee trouble. Use discretion in deciding whether or not to do it.)

a.

b.

7. Pushing and kicking the legs. While lying on your back, kick your legs with the feeling that you are pushing a wall with your heels. This is slightly different from the so-called bicycle motion.

a.

b.

8. Running and skipping rope. In addition to doing the above exercises, those people who want to attain the strength of a superbly conditioned athlete are advised to run or jog regularly (at least two or three miles at a time). Skipping rope is also quite effective for body conditioning (five to fifteen minutes every day).

a.

b.

2

Twelve lessons on basic self-defense techniques

As has been made clear in the Introduction, this book concerns itself primarily with the elements of self-defense techniques that are necessary, effective, and meaningful, and *not* with formal karate as an art-sport. However, it seems quite important that a person who wishes to become proficient in the art of self-defense should be acquainted with the basic techniques of karate. Therefore, throughout the lessons basic karate techniques and their applications are explained.

Lesson 1

A. The natural stance. The natural stance is formed by standing with your two feet a shoulder width apart, as shown below. Relax your shoulders and keep your back straight, with the feeling that the stomach is slightly outward. As its name suggests, this is an easy stance. It is used as a preparatory stance for the practice of self-defense. You must learn how to shift your body right to left, and, back and forth, from this basic stance.

1.

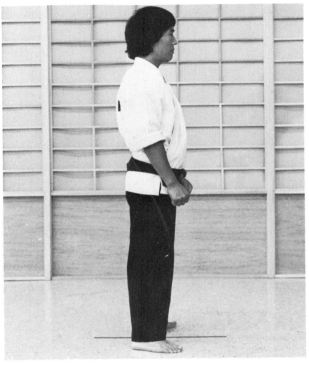

2.

B. Fists. It is extremely important to have a good fist whenever it is needed in either defensive or offensive techniques. In the normal fist, there are two methods of folding the fingers. Both methods are equally effective, but the one with the index finger bent inward is more widely used than the one with the index finger kept straight while pressed by the thumb. Let's, for the sake of clarification, call the former the *a* method, and the latter, which is older, the *b* method.

Making a fist: method *a*. Follow photos 1 to 4, step by step.

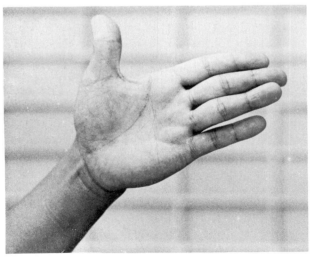

1.

2.

3.

4.

5. A side view of the fist at the moment of thrusting.

6. A front view of the fist at the moment of thrusting.

Making a fist: method *b*. Follow photos 1 to 4,
step by step.

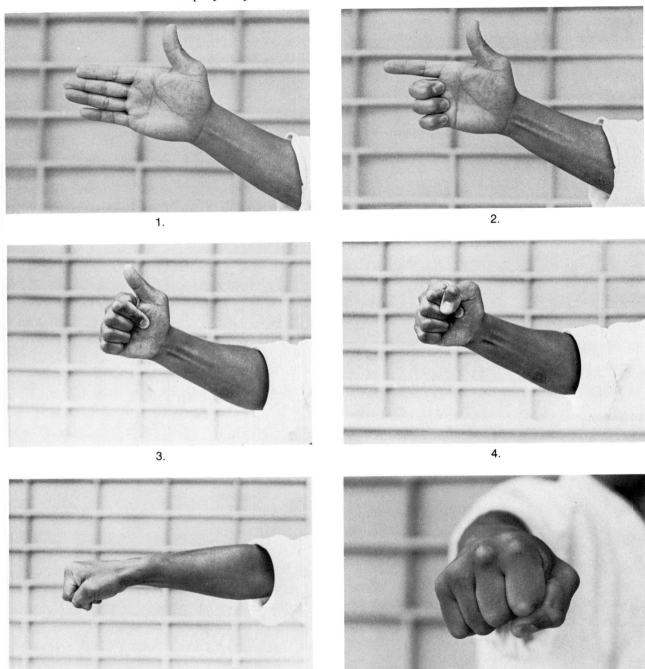

1.

2.

3.

4.

5. A side view of the fist at the moment of thrusting.

6. A front view of the fist at the moment of thrusting.

Note: The most important thing to remember in making a fist is to bend the fingers each time in sufficient degree. In using the fist, it must be kept in mind that the point of contact to targets is the back of the first two knuckles. The back of the wrist is kept straight, as shown in the above photos.

C. Punching. Basically, karate punches are thrust according to a simple law of geometry: the shortest distance between two points is a straight line.

1. Assume the natural stance with both fists on the sides of your hips, showing the palm side of the fists upward.
2. Bring both fists forward until the elbows come to the point of leaving the side of the body.
3. As the elbows pass the side of the body, start to straighten them as you twist the fists to reach the target with the palm sides facing downward.

At this time, let us focus our fists on the point straight ahead of your own solar plexus. Follow photos 1 to 5 step by step in slow motion. This is preliminary practice for the punching method.

1.

2.

3.

4.

5.

4. After you have repeated the above-mentioned preliminary practice movements for a sufficient number of times, leave the left fist where it is at the point straight ahead of your solar plexus and pull back the right fist to the right side of your hip. (At this time, we concentrate on thrusting at the midsection of the body as the target.)

5. Then, as you thrust the right fist, bring back the left fist to the side of the left hip as shown in the photos below. The action of the two arms, thrusting and pulling, should be synchronized. Let's try it very slowly in the beginning, without any speed or power, and later we will add these elments as you progress.

Note: In order to thrust your punch in the most effective way, you must remember to throw your thrusting arm along the side of your hip rather tightly (let your elbow rub as you thrust) so that your fist can travel the shortest distance to the target.

Follow photos 6 to 10 step by step.

6.

7.

8.

9

10.

Note: Theoretically, three major divisions in the human body serve as targets: the upper part, which is above the neck (its front center is the point below the nose); the midsection (the center of which is the solar plexus; the lower part (the center of which is the groin). For details of these vital points in the human body, please refer to Chapter 4 of this book.

Now, let's practice the other arm (thrusting with the left arm and pulling back the right arm). Follow photos 11 to 14.

11.

12.

13.

14.

For your reference, the following photos illustrate a side view of the right-arm punching motions.

15.

16.

17.

18.

19.

20.

Note: During the entire motion of punching, your shoulders must be relaxed and the punching power must emanate from the lower abdomen with ki-a-i.

D. The downward block. The downward block can be applied against an opponent's attack to your midsection and/or your groin.

1. Assume the natural stance and bring the left hand to the right shoulder with its palm side facing upward.

2. As you slide the left fist down along the right arm, twist it so that its palm side faces downward at the moment the block is completed. First, let's practice the block without worrying about the other arm. Follow photos 1 to 6 carefully and slowly.

1.

2.

3.

4.

5.

6.

3. After you repeat the above-mentioned movements several times, you can proceed to the next movements. As you block downward with your right arm, pull your left hand back to the side of your hip. Follow photos 7 to 11 slowly.

7.

8.

9.

10.

11.

12. After completing the block, execute the middle punch with the left arm, as shown here.

Note: Repeat the whole series of movements with the left arm as the blocking arm. Execute the right punch at the completion of the block.

E. Application of the downward block against the one-wrist grab

1. Suppose that your opponent grabs your right wrist.
2. Bring your left fist to your right shoulder to prepare for the downward block.
3. As you block downward with your left arm according to the method described earlier, hit your opponent's left wrist to take it off your wrist, and at the same time, pull back the right fist to the side of your hip.
4. Follow the blocking action immediately with the right punch to your opponent's face.

Follow photos 1 to 6 carefully in slow motion.

1.

2.

3.

4.

5.

6.

Note: If you do not have a partner available, just use the concept of the imaginary opponent. The same point applies to all of the other techniques that are explained in this book. Also, it is extremely important that you practice every technique on both the right and left sides.

Lesson 2

Lesson 1 was inevitably very basic without much variety, and some of you may have found it a little boring. We can assure you that it will become more interesting and challenging if you stay with it. Also, don't forget that basic techniques are the foundation of your future progress, so be sure to review Lesson 1 before you move on to Lesson 2. Before you move on to any new lesson be sure to review the previous lesson.

A. Defense against the one-wrist grab: method *a*
   1. In the same way as in the preceding situation, your opponent grabs your wrist (this time the left one).
   2. You can do several things to deal with this situation. Here we will discuss the most basic method. Twist your left wrist counterclockwise, and immediately grab your opponent's grabbing hand at the wrist.
   3. Bring your right foot close to your opponent's, and as you press down his right hand with your left hand, apply upward pressure behind your opponent's right elbow with your right forearm.

1.

2.

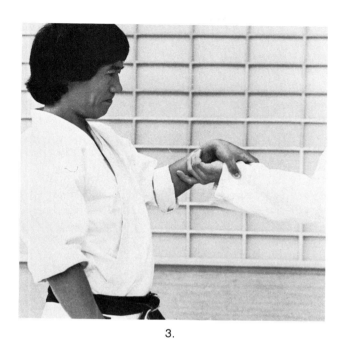

3.

4.

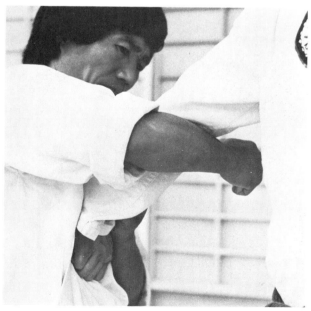

6.

5. When you feel it necessary, you can throw a short and quick punch to your opponent's midsection before you apply pressure to the back of your opponent's elbow.

7.

8. When your technique is effective, your opponent stands on the balls of his feet and loses freedom of movement.

B. Defense against the one-wrist grab: method *b*

1. As your opponent grabs your left wrist with his right hand, twist your left wrist counterclockwise and immediately grab his right wrist. (And if necessary, execute an attack to your opponent's face with a palm-heel strike.)
2. Bend your opponent's right arm backward with your two hands, and rotate your whole body with it.
3. Step forward with your left foot and take down your opponent to his back.

Follow photos 1 to 10 step by step. In applying any self-defense technique, you must depend on the scientific aspects of the technique instead of relying on brute force to make the technique work. A good, systematic technique is based on scientific principles, and if you follow those principles closely, after enough practice you should be able to execute the technique without awkward forcefulness.

1.

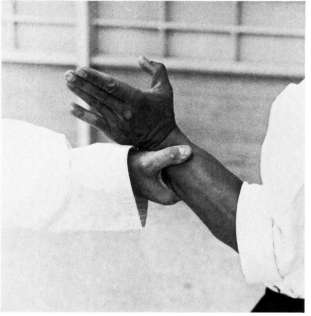

2.

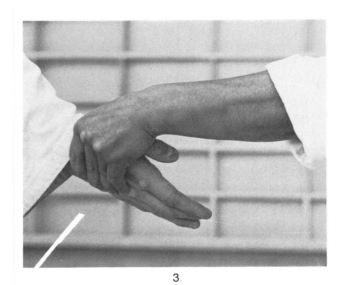

3.

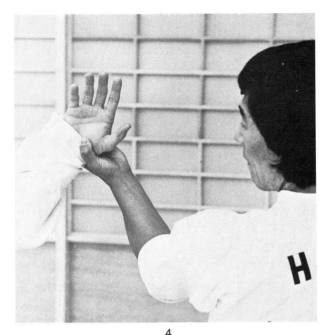

4.

5.

6.

7.

8.

9.

10. When you hold onto your opponent's wrists with two hands as you throw him, this technique becomes a submission hold, as shown here.

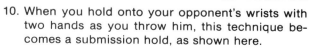

C. Defense against the cross-wrist grab
1. Your opponent grabs your right wrist with his right hand, as shown below.
2. Bring your left foot forward, simultaneously clapping your hands to enforce the power of your right arm, which you are about to twist clockwise.
3. As soon as you twist your clapped hands to the extent that you are able to grab your opponent's right wrist with your right hand, let your left hand go and start to apply pressure behind your opponent's right elbow.
4. Pull your opponent's right arm forward and downward with your right hand while you maintain pressure on the back of your opponent's right elbow.
5. As you complete your opponent's submission, place his right forearm deep onto your right thigh and maintain strong pressure behind his right elbow.

Follow photos 1 to 6 carefully.

1. Your right wrist is being grabbed by your opponent's right hand.

2. At this moment, you move your left foot forward, outside your opponent's right foot.

3.

4. You then apply pressure with your left forearm on the back of your opponent's right elbow.

5.

6.

7. When your opponent is so strong that you find it difficult to achieve his submission by applying pressure to the back of his elbow, hold the side of your front ankle with the arm that is applying the pressure. The stabler and stronger force that this gives you may enable you to apply enough pressure to the back of your opponent's elbow to achieve his submission.

Note: In this particular takedown technique, your front foot is not next to his head. It is always the one away from your opponent's position. In other words, if you are taking the opponent by giving pressure to his right elbow, then your front foot is the right one; while, if you are taking him down by his left arm, then your front foot is your left one. Make sure that you practice both right and left sides.

For your reference, photos 8 to 11 illustrate how this defense is applied if your opponent grabs your left wrist.

8.

9.

10.

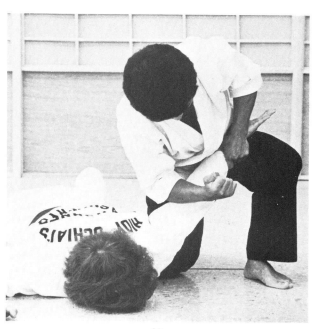

11.

Lesson 3

A. The upper block

    1. Assume the natural stance, and bring your blocking arm (practice with your left arm first) to the left side of your hip in the same way as you do in preparing for punching.

    2. Ignore your right arm for the moment, and concentrate on your left, blocking arm only.

    3. Bring your left fist up with its palm side facing toward you, and aim your fist to your right shoulder area.

    4. When your fist comes to the area above your right shoulder, twist it so that the palm side faces your opponent and so that the elbow of your blocking arm comes up at the end of the block.

1.

2.

3.

4.

5.

6.

5. Repeat the whole motion until you feel comfortable with it and then utilize your other arm—your right arm—as the pulling force. In the upper block as illustrated in photos 7 to 12, the pulling arm is inside and the blocking arm travels outside.

7.

8.

9.

10

11.

12.

Note: In executing an upper block, it is important not to let the elbow of the blocking arm come up too early. At the completion of the block with a twisting motion of the fist, the elbow should come up in a natural way.

6. Practice the upper block with a partner if one is available. Ask your partner to attack your face from a prearranged position, and then block your partner's attack. At first, have your partner attack you slowly. Later, he or she can gradually execute stronger and faster attacks.

13.

14.

B. The front stance. In an actual self-defense situation, it is unlikely that you will utilize the formal front stance. However, the front stance is valuable in developing strong hips and good balance as a whole, and during your practice you should try to apply it according to its proper use.

1. Weight distribution is about 60/40. That is, you place about 60 percent of your weight on your front foot and 40 percent on your back foot.

2. The length of the stance is kept at two natural footsteps; the width is that of your shoulder.

3. Keep your front foot pointing forward and your back foot facing forward at 45 degrees.

1.

2.

4. The length of a minor front stance is one natural footstep. In an actual self-defense situation, you may utilize the minor front stance more often than the normal one.

3.

4.

C. The lunge punch. This punch is executed with the arm that is on the same side as the forward foot.

   1. From the natural stance, extend the arm that will become the pulling arm. Step forward, and execute the punch with the arm that is on the same side as the forward foot.

1.

2.

2. Block your opponent's attack with your left arm and as your opponent steps back, chase him with a lunging motion of the

right foot and simultaneously execute the right-lunge attack.

3.

4. After you block, your opponent steps back.

5. Now you lunge toward your opponent.

6. You deliver the upper lunge punch.

Note: Realistically speaking, the lunge punch as it has been presented here may have no practical value. In other words, in an actual self-defence situation you would not expect your opponent to step back immediately after your first block instead of executing a second and third attack. In the study of any martial art,

however, so-called grammatical form situations have been developed for the sake of effective practice. The situation presented here has been used in order to enable you to learn the lunge punch with an actual partner. Many of the self-defense techniques that follow will be presented in a similar manner.

D. The crescent walk. In formal karate training, we emphasize and practice the so-called crescent walk, but it is not necessary to practice the walk if your only purpose is to develop self-defense techniques. This method of proceeding forward is impractical in actual fighting, for it slows your movements. However, the crescent walk helps you to acquire the concept of the center of gravity, which is directly related to your sense of balance.

1. Take a full front stance.

2. Bring the back foot both forward and inward. Keep the right knee bent.

3. As you make a crescent form with the proceeding foot, bring the foot outward.

4. Complete the step as you form another front stance, with the stepping foot finishing the crescent form.

Note: The important thing to learn from the crescent walk is that you must keep the height of your hip from the floor constant during the stepping motion (that is, your center of gravity must be kept at the same level all the time).

E. The half-and-half stance. In blocking situations, the natural stance does not give you enough stability when you receive the impact of an attack. Under these circumstances the front stance is not too suitable for blocking either, though it is often used in blocking during prearranged sparring practice in karate training. Therefore, you are about to be introduced to the stance called the half-and-half stance, which is used primarily for blocking.

1. In making the half-and-half stance, you distribute 50 percent of your weight on each foot and you open your feet to the same distance as you do for the front stance.

1.

2.

2. According to your preference and the situations, you may use the "minor" half-and-half stance shown in photos 3 and 4.

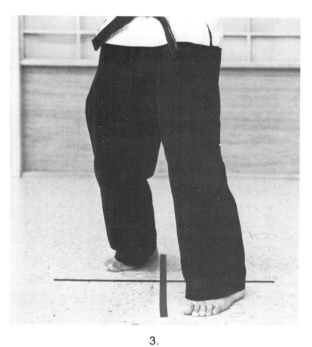

3.

4.

F. The reverse punch. This punch is thrust by the right hand with the left foot forward, and vice versa.

1.

2.

1. Your opponent attacks you with his right upper punch, which you block by stepping back on your right foot, thus making the left half-and-half stance.

2. After you block, you shift your weight onto your front foot (the left foot in this case) by stretching the right back knee. By so doing, you are rotating your hip and trunk toward your punching arm (the right reverse punch is used in this case).

3

4.

3. As usual, make sure to practice with the other arm as well.

5.

6.

G. Comparison between the lunge punch and the reverse punch.

 1. In reach, the lunge punch is superior to the reverse punch, as shown in photos 1 and 2.

From the same distance, the reverse punch falls short and the lunge punch reaches.

1. The reverse punch falls short.

2. The lunge punch reaches.

3.

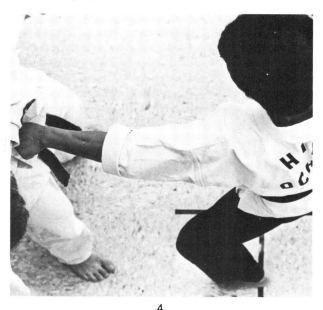

4.

 2. In balance, the reverse punch is normally superior.
 3. Because of stronger rotation of the hip and the trunk, as well as the possibility of better focus, the reverse punch normally produces greater power. Consequently, in breaking techniques, for example, the reverse punch is normally used.

Lesson 4

A. The outer major sweep: method *a*

1. Block your opponent's right upper attack with your left arm by stepping back with your right foot.

2. As you grab your opponent's attacking arm with your left hand, step forward slightly, placing your left foot next to your opponent's right foot.

3. Attack the left side of your opponent's chin with your open right hand.

4. Keep holding your opponent's right arm under your left armpit, and bring your right foot behind your opponent's right leg.

5. Now you are ready to execute the outer major sweep. At the moment of sweeping, three forces must be synchronized: (*a*) your left arm pulls down your opponent's right arm; (*b*) your open right hand pushes the left side of your opponent's chin; and (*c*) your right foot sweeps your opponent's right foot.

1. Block your opponent's right upper attack with your left arm.

2. Grab your opponent's attacking arm with your left hand, and step with your left foot outside your opponent's right foot.

3. Attack the left side of your opponent's chin with your open right hand as you bring your opponent's right arm toward you.

4. Bring your right foot behind your opponent's right foot, and place it so that your right calf makes contact with your opponent's right calf.

6. As you sweep your opponent's leg, make sure that you keep holding your opponent's arm very tightly, and at the same time keep pushing with your open right hand on the side of your opponent's chin.

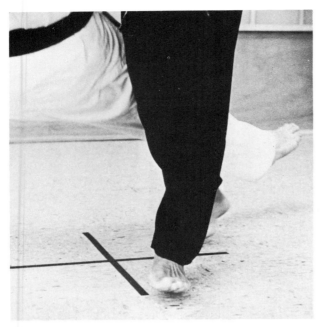

7. The ball of your sweeping foot should make a kind of circular motion on the floor.

8. When your opponent falls to the ground, you should keep holding onto his arm.

Let's look at the technique from another view.

9. This is the moment when you step with your left foot outside your opponent's right foot and you keep your open right hand on the left side of your opponent's chin.

10. Here you have moved your right foot behind your opponent's right foot and you are about to throw your opponent.

11. At this moment your opponent has fallen to the floor.

12. In an actual self-defense situation, after having completed this technique, you may or may not execute the final attack shown here.

B. The outer major sweep: method *b*

1. Execute the right upper block against your opponent's right upper attack by stepping back with your left foot and forming a half-and-half stance.

2. Step forward with your left foot next to your opponent's right foot, and push down your opponent's attacking arm with your left hand.

3. As with method *a*, attack the left side of your opponent's chin with your open right hand, and then bring your right foot behind your opponent's right foot to prepare for sweeping.

4. Now you are ready to execute the outer major sweep. At the moment of throwing, the only difference between method *a* and method *b* is that in method *b* you do not hold your opponent's attacking arm under your left armpit. Instead, you simply grab it and pull it downward as you sweep.

Follow photos 1 to 6 step by step carefully.

1. Block your opponent's right upper attack with your right arm by stepping back with your left foot and forming a half-and-half stance.

2. Immediately, try to grab your opponent's attacking arm with your left hand. This step already begins the step shown in photo 3.

3. As you move forward with your left foot, push down your opponent's attacking arm with your left hand. This prevents your opponent from making a second attack with his other arm (his left arm in this case).

4. Attack the left side of your opponent's chin with your right hand (the palm heel), and thus break your opponent's balance completely.

5. From this point, the same things can be said of method *b* as have been said of method *a*. In executing your method *b* outer major sweep, make sure to synchronize the three forces that we mentioned in our discussion of method *a*.

6.

Note: It goes without saying that you must practice this technique, like any other technique, from both the right side and the left side.

C. The "open block" and the "closed block"
  1. As in method *a* of the outer major sweep,
      blocking your opponent's right hand at-
      tack with your left arm or blocking your
      opponent's left hand attack with your
      right arm is called an "open block."

1. Open block.

2. Open block.

  2. As in method *b* of the outer major sweep,
      blocking your opponent's right hand at-
      tack with your right hand, and vice
      versa, is called a "closed block."

3. Closed block against your opponent's right upper
   punch.

4. Closed downward block against your opponent's
   right middle attack.

Lesson 5

A. The outside-inside middle block. Although the downward block (which you learned in Lesson 1) is adequate against the middle attack, it is useful and convenient to be familiar with the outside-inside middle block.

1. Assume the natural stance, with your right blocking arm in the ready position.
2. Without changing the face of your right fist, bring it to your midsection.
3. At the moment of blocking, change the direction of your right fist to show its palm side upward, and drop your right elbow to complete the block.

First, let's practice this without worrying about the pulling arm.

1.

2.

3.

4.

Now let's practice the same block with a pulling motion of the other arm. Follow photos 5 to 8 step by step. In the beginning, it's important to go through this very slowly, without any power. Later on, you can add speed and power to your technique.

5.

6.

7.

8.

Note: In this technique it is extremely important to drop the elbow of the blocking arm at the very end of the execution of the block. (Practice both the right side and the left side patiently.)

B. The straddle stance. You are unlikely to use this particular stance in an actual self-defense situation. However, this is an important stance to practice for the development of strength in the hips and the legs.
1. The distance between the two feet is approximately two shoulder widths.
2. Point both feet slightly inward, bend the knees sufficiently, and force both knees slightly outward.
3. Keep the back straight.

1

2.

3. You can make a minor straddle stance by shortening the distance between the two feet as shown here.

4.

C. The side-elbow strike

1. You can practice the side-elbow strike from the natural stance position as shown. In the preparatory position, the fist is palm side upward. When the execution of the side-elbow strike has been completed, the fist is palm side downward.

1. In this preparatory position, the fist of the executing arm is palm side upward.

2.

3. At the completion of the side-elbow strike, the fist of the executing arm is palm side downward.

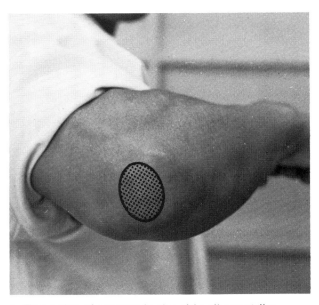

4. The point of contact in the side-elbow strike.

2. The straddle stance imparts greater power and stability to the execution of the side elbow strike.

1.

2.

3.

4.

Note: Of course, in the beginning you may practice the side elbow strike without the motion of the pulling arm.

D. Application of the side elbow strike
   1. Block your opponent's middle attack with your right inside-outside middle block as you form a half-and-half stance.
   2. Grab your opponent's attacking arm with your left hand, and pull your right arm to prepare for the execution of the side elbow strike.
   3. By adjusting both feet slightly, and thus making the straddle stance, execute the right side elbow strike to your opponent's midsection.

Follow photos 1 to 4 step by step. Practice slowly at first, and then gradually increase your speed and power.

1.

2.

3.

4.

4. Practice the other side as well.

E. The back-elbow strike
1. You may practice the back-elbow strike from various stances. Suppose that we practice it from the minor half-and-half stance.
2. Extend completely the arm that you are about to use for the back-elbow strike, and pull the arm as you twist it to the side of your hip. In other words, this is the reverse of the punching process.

1.

2.

3.

4.

You can also practice the back-elbow strike effectively with the straddle stance.

5.

6.

F. Application of the back-elbow strike

1. As with the side elbow strike, first execute your right outside-inside middle block with the half-and-half stance.
2. Grab your opponent's attacking arm with your blocking arm (your right arm in this case), and at the same time bring your right foot in front of your opponent's right foot as you prepare your left arm for the back elbow strike by extending the arm.

3. As you pull back your left foot inside your opponent's left foot, execute the left elbow attack to your opponent's solar plexus or ribs.
4. Remember to practice the back elbow strike step by step slowly in the beginning, then with gradually increasing speed and power.

1. Block your opponent's attack.

2. Grab your opponent's attacking arm.

3. Prepare for the execution of the back elbow strike.

4. Complete the back elbow strike to your opponent's solar plexus.

Let's look at this technique, especially the last
two movements, from another view.

5. You are ready to execute the back elbow strike.

6. This is the moment at which you complete the back elbow strike to your opponent's solar plexus area.

7. Throughout the technique, you keep holding your opponent's first attacking arm tightly.

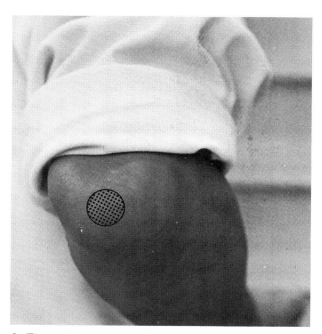

8. The point of contact in the back elbow strike.

Lesson 6

A. The straight back-fist strike
1. Assume the natural stance, and bring both fists in front of your chest.
2. Stretch both arms to the imaginary target, which should be at your eye level, and snap back the elbows without twisting the fists. The whole maneuver should be executed with a strong snapping movement of the elbows.

1. Assume the ready position, with both arms in front of your chest.

2. Let your fists travel straight to the target without twisting them.

3. The moment of completing the double back-fist strike. The back of the first two knuckles makes contact with the target.

4. Snap your fists back immediately after completing the attack.

B. Application of the straight back-fist strike:
   method *a*
   1. Suppose that your opponent grabs both
      your wrists.
   2. Step forward with either of your feet, and
      at the same time twist both fists against
      your opponent's thumbs.
   3. After taking off your opponent's grab-
      bing hands, throw the back-fist strike
      straight to your opponent's eyes.

Follow photos 1 to 6 step by step.

1.

2.

3.

4.

5.

6.

Photos 7 and 8 show how you free your wrists from your opponent's grabbing by twisting them against your opponent's thumbs.

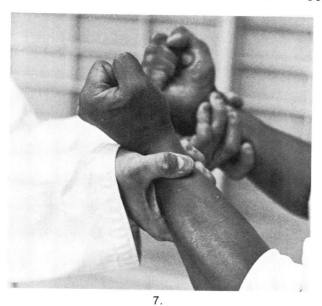

7.

8.

C. Application of the straight back-fist strike: method *b*

1. After you block your opponent's upper attack, keep your blocking arm in place and prepare to execute the straight back-fist strike with the other arm.

2. Shifting your weight slightly forward, execute the straight back-fist strike to your opponent's face (below the nose or directly to an eye).

1.

2.

3.

4. Execute the back-fist strike to your opponent's face below the nose. (The eyes are also a good target.)

D. The up-and-down back-fist strike

1. Assume the natural stance, with your right hand high above your shoulder and your left arm extended so as to be ready for the pulling motion.
2. As you twist your right fist, strike the target with the up-and-down motion.

Your point of contact with the target is the back of the first two knuckles.
3. Pull back your other arm to the side of your hip as you execute the up-and-down back-fist strike.

1.

2.

3.

4.

E. Application of the up-and-down back-fist
   strike

1. After you block your opponent's right
   upper attack with your left upper block,
   grab your opponent's attacking arm immediately with your blocking arm.
2. At the same time, raise your right fist
   high, palm side downward, to be ready

for your up-and-down back-fist strike to
your opponent's face.
3. Strike down your right back fist as you
   twist it on your opponent's face as you
   keep grabbing your opponent's right
   arm.

1.

2.

3.

4.

Let's look at this technique from another angle with a close-up.

5.

6.

7.

8.

Note: It is important to bear in mind that, in the offensive sense, there are basically two methods of utilizing your hands: punching and striking. Punching is executed straight to a target, whereas striking can be executed from different directions in basically three ways: straight back fist, up-and-down back fist, and roundhouse back fist.

F. The roundhouse back-fist strike
   1. From the same position as is used in punching, bring your fist forward as you pull your other arm to the side of your hip.
   2. As you throw your fist forward, twist it in such a way that the first two knuckles make contact with the target.
   3. As with other back-fist strikes, it is important to pull back the attacking arm immediately.

1.

2.

3.

4.

Note: The roundhouse back-fist strike is normally used to focus the attack on the opponent's temple or on the side of the opponent's body, at points which you cannot reach by a straight attack.

G. Application of the roundhouse back-fist strike

1. Your opponent tries to attack your face with his right hand while covering the front side of his face with his left hand so that you cannot counterattack directly from the front side.

2. After blocking with your left arm, grab your opponent's attacking right arm with your blocking arm.

3. As you press down your opponent's right arm, throw the right roundhouse back-fist strike to your opponent's temple.

1.

2.

3.

4.

As with the other techniques, let's practice
this one from different sides.

5.

6.

7.

8.

Lesson 7

A. The one-middle-knuckle fist. One of the most effective attacking weapons is the one-middle-knuckle fist. Not much strength is required to make this fist effective if the fist is executed on the right targets, such as the ribs, the temple, the eyes, and the face.

1. To form the one-middle-knuckle fist, push the middle-finger knuckle out and after the middle finger is bent, squeeze it with the index finger and the ring finger.

2. Make sure that the middle knuckle will not be pushed down when it hits the target. In order to ensure that this won't happen, hold the ring finger and the index finger together and close the thumb tightly.

1.

2.

3.

B. Application of the one-middle-knuckle fist. This fist can be used effectively to attack your opponent's ribs, eyes, and temples, his face below the nose, and so on.

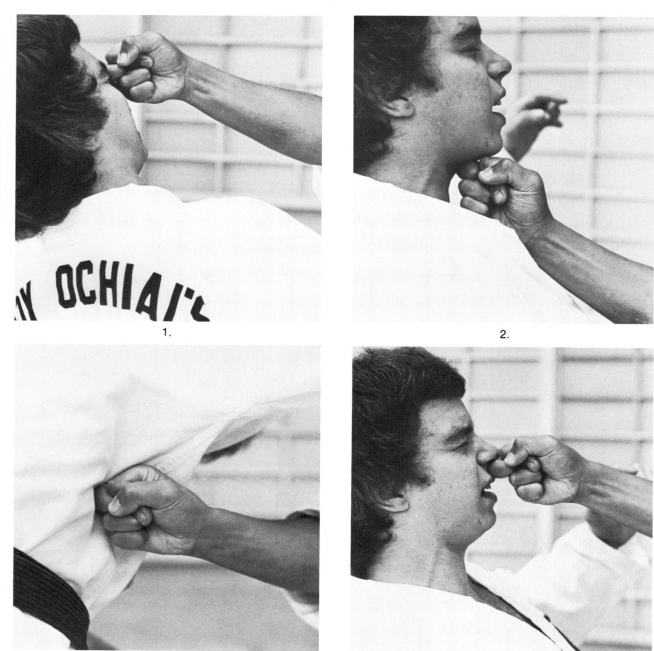

1.

2.

3.

4.

Note: The one-middle-knuckle fist may be executed in the same manner as that used in the normal punching method, or you can simply thrust the fist straight without any twisting motion.

C. The index-finger-knuckle fist
   1. Place the thumb inside the index finger.
   2. Push the index-finger knuckle out as the thumb pushes it out. The other fingers are all bent inward tightly, just as with a normal fist. Follow photos 1 to 4 step by step to form a proper index-finger-knuckle fist.

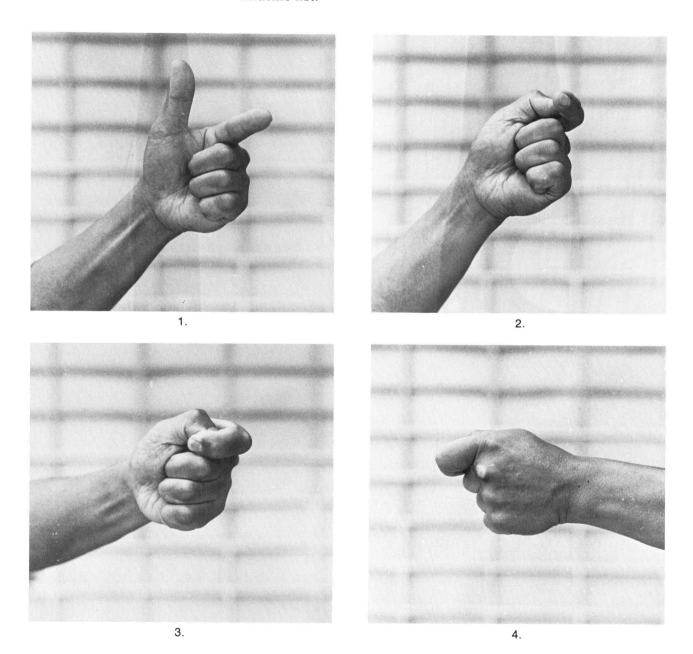

1.

2.

3.

4.

Note: The index-finger-knuckle fist can be applied in the same way as the one-middle-knuckle fist.

D. The front-elbow strike. Although you need to be in close proximity to your opponent to execute elbow strikes effectively, such strikes can be very devastating. If you are practicing with a partner, make sure that you control your elbow attacks 100 percent so that you do not hurt the partner. Of course, when you practice with a partner, this rule of control is very important in all techniques, and it should be strictly obeyed.

1. The front-elbow strike starts from the same position as the reverse punch.
2. Bring your attacking arm (your right arm in this case) along the side of your hip, and as its elbow passes your body, change the direction of your fist to the left side of your body.
3. Then, push out your elbow to the target as you complete turning your fist and bringing your arm across the midsection of your body.
4. As shown in photos 1 to 7, the front-elbow strike, like the reverse punch, is practiced most effectively from the half-and-half stance.

Follow photos 1 to 5 step by step, first slowly and then gradually with more power and speed.

1.

2.

3.

4.

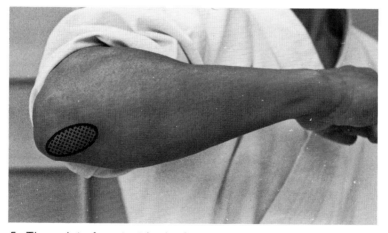

5. The point of contact in the front-elbow strike.

6. Let's look at the front-elbow strike from the side.

7.

8.

9.

Note: Practice the front-elbow strike with both the right arm and the left arm. In the beginning, you may practice the front-elbow strike from the natural stance position.

E. Application of the front-elbow strike

1. Block your opponent's right upper block with your right arm (in other words, use the closed block).
2. As you step forward with your left foot to the outside of your opponent's right foot, push down on your opponent's attacking arm.

3. With full rotation of your hip and trunk behind your executing arm, complete the right front-elbow strike to your opponent's midsection.

1.

2.

3.

4.

F. The upper-elbow strike
  1. Like the front-elbow strike, the upper-elbow strike starts with the fist of your executing arm on the side of your hip.
  2. Bring your fist upward without changing the facing of the fist.
  3. After your elbow passes your body, twist your fist to turn its palm side toward your right temple and throw the end point of your elbow to your opponent's chin.

1.　　　2.

3.　　　4.

Note: Like many other techniques, the upper-elbow strike can easily be practiced from the natural stance position.

Let's look at the upper-elbow strike from another view.

5.

6.

7.

8.

G. Application of the upper-elbow strike
   1. You block your opponent's upper attack with the open block position (that is, if your opponent attacks you with his right arm, you block with your left arm, and vice versa). Shown in photos 1 to 4 is the case in which you block your opponent's right arm attack with your left arm.
   2. As soon as you block, grab your opponent's attacking arm with your blocking arm. Your other arm is then ready to execute the upper-elbow attack.
   3. While you pull your opponent's arm strongly under your armpit, execute the upper-elbow attack to your opponent's chin.

1.

2.

3.

4.

H. The knife-hand strike
1. As shown in photos 1 and 2, the thumb is bent inward tightly.
2. The other four fingers are bent inward very slightly.
3. The point of contact with the target is shown in photos 1 and 2.

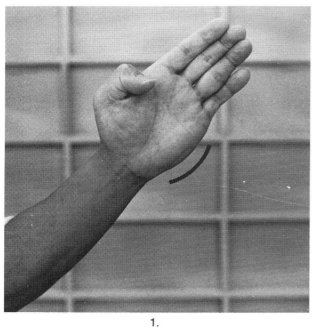

1.

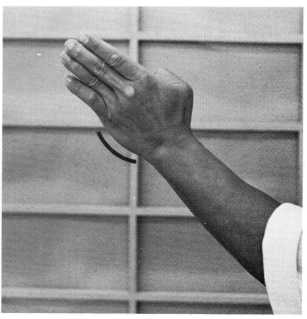

2.

I. Application of the knife-hand strike: method *a*

1. As you block your opponent's right middle attack with your right outside-inward block, immediately grab your opponent's attacking right arm with your left hand while your right arm is raised high so as to be ready for the delivery of the knife-hand attack.

2. Your knife hand must come down with a twisting motion for greater power to the target.

1. Block your opponent's attack with the half-and-half stance.

2. Grab your opponent's attacking arm with your left hand, while your right hand is ready for the knife-hand attack.

3. Make sure that your knife-hand strike is delivered with a twisting motion.

4. Here the knife-hand is executed on the side of your opponent's neck.

J. Application of the knife-hand strike: method *b*

1. Block your opponent's right upper attack with your left arm.

2. Immediately, your right arm is raised high to the ready position for delivering the knife-hand attack to the side of your opponent's neck.

3. Make sure that you keep holding onto your opponent's right arm as you execute the right knife-hand strike.

1.

2.

3.

4.

K. Application of the knife-hand strike: method *c*

1. Block your opponent's right upper attack with your right arm (the closed block).
2. Grab your opponent's attacking arm with your blocking arm, and pull your opponent's attacking arm down as you adjust your right foot slightly.
3. Bring your left knife hand up, with the palm side facing upward.
4. Deliver your left knife hand directly your opponent's throat. Again, make sure that you control your attack 100 percent during practice with your partner. (The stance at the last moment is the minor straddle stance.)

1.

2.

3.

4.

Lesson 8

A. The front kick. This is probably the easiest of the kicking techniques because it requires a very natural muscle coordination. Depending on how you use the front kick, it can also be one of the most effective self-defense weapons.

1. First, lift your kicking foot to your knee level.
2. Thrust your kicking foot forward with the toes curled up, so that the ball of the foot makes contact with the target.
3. Make sure that your supporting foot is stable, with its knee slightly bent.
4. At the moment you kick, your power must come from your lower abdomen with a strong exhalation of air. (See the discussion of ki-a-i in the Introduction.)

Follow photos 1 to 4 slowly at first, then with gradually increasing power and speed. (If you have bad knees, use your own discretion in practicing kicking techniques.)

1.

2.

3.

4.

Note: The important thing is not how high you can kick, but how well and how strongly with focus you can execute the kicking techniques.

5.

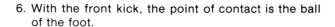

6. With the front kick, the point of contact is the ball of the foot.

5. In order to learn how to execute the front kick properly, with a thrusting motion, you should practice how to thrust your heel out. At the moment you execute the front kick with heel, you must throw your whole hip outward for greater power.

7.

8.

9.

10.

11. A high front-thrust kick with heel.

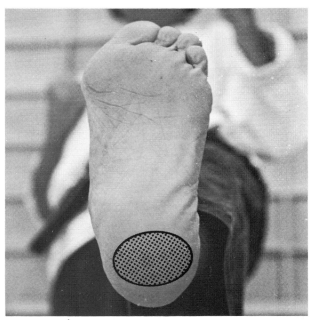

12. The point of contact of the front-thrust kick with heel.

Note: One of the most important things to remember in executing front kicks is to pull back the kicking foot immediately after its contact with the target. This is done to prevent your opponent from grabbing your kicking foot and also for the sake of keeping good balance all the time. The supporting foot must be stable, with the knee slightly bent for better stability.

B. Application of the front kick: method *a*

1. Block your opponent's right upper attack with your right arm (closed block), and grab your opponent's attacking arm immediately with both your hands as you pull back your right foot slightly to adjust the distance and at the same time to break your opponent's balance.

2. As you keep holding your opponent's right arm with both your hands, deliver the front kick to your opponent's groin, solar plexus, or ribs.

1. Block the upper attack with the natural stance. (This movement can also be practiced effectively with the half-and-half stance.)

2. Grab your opponent's arm and pull it, and at the same time make a stepping-back motion with your right foot.

3. Make sure that you raise your kicking foot (the left foot here) to your knee level.

4. Thrust the front kick to your opponent's midsection (a front kick to the floating rib area can be most effective).

C. Application of the front kick: method *b*
   1. Block your opponent's right upper attack with your left arm.
   2. As in the method *a* application of the front kick, pull your opponent's attacking arm slightly forward to break his balance and at the same time to adjust the distance for your front kick.
   3. Deliver a high front kick to your opponent's chin.

Note: As always, practice with both sides of the body, and during practice with your partner, remember to employ full control so that neither you nor your partner hurt each other by mistake.

1.

2.

3.

4.

D. Application of the front kick: method *c*

1. Your opponent approaches you with a knife in his hand.
2. Watch the distance carefully, and when your opponent comes to the area where you can reach him with your foot, deliver a fast and strong front kick to your opponent's groin with a snapping motion.
3. Grab the hand with the weapon immediately, and subdue.

1. Watch the distance that separates you from your opponent.

2. When you find a proper opening, deliver a strong, sudden front kick to your opponent's groin.

3. Grab the hand in which your opponent is holding the knife.

4. Take the knife away from your opponent.

E. The roundhouse kick. When used correctly, the roundhouse kick is very effective, since it contains an element of surprising counter-attack.

1. Raise your kicking foot high to your side while bending the knee completely.
2. Thrust your kicking foot around forward, almost parallel to the floor. (Of course, you cannot throw your kicking foot parallel to the floor if you mean to kick very high or very low. But initially, for the sake of practice, it is good to do this.)
3. Again, it is important to pull back your kicking foot immediately. Make sure that your supporting foot turns about 90 degrees back and forth as you kick and then pull back your kicking foot.
4. The ball of the foot is generally utilized as the kicking point. However, it is also possible to use the instep as the kicking point, especially in kicking your opponent's temple.

1. The ready position for the roundhouse kick.

2. Raise your kicking foot high, with the knee completely bent.

3.

4. As you deliver the roundhouse kick, the stable supporting foot turns about 90 degrees.

5. Let's look at the roundhouse kick from another angle.

6.

7.

8.

9. A high roundhouse kick.

10.

F. Application of the roundhouse kick: method *a*

1. When you receive an upper attack, dodge it to your left if the attack is by a right arm, and vice versa.
2. Grab your opponent's attacking arm immediately, and execute the right roundhouse kick to your opponent's solar plexus, groin, and/or temple. (Execute the left roundhouse kick if your opponent attacks with a left punch.) As you deliver the roundhouse kick, you had better keep holding onto your opponent's arm as shown.

1. Dodge your opponent's right upper attack by stepping to your left slightly with your left foot.

2. Grab your opponent's attacking arm immediately. Here the right roundhouse kick is being delivered to the opponent's groin.

3. This roundhouse kick is being delivered to the opponent's solar plexus.

4. You attack your opponent's temple with your instep, although you can use the ball of the foot as well.

Let's look at the roundhouse kicks from a different angle. (Of course, you must practice the roundhouse kicks with both the right foot and the left foot.)

5. Grab your opponent's left attacking arm, and you are ready to deliver the roundhouse kick.

6. The roundhouse kick to your opponent's groin.

7. The roundhouse kick to your opponent's solar plexus area. You can use the instep to the midsection also, though it may be less effective than the ball of the foot.

8. The instep roundhouse kick to your opponent's temple.

Note: Again, you must keep in mind that what is important is *not* how high you can kick but how correctly and effectively you can focus your kick on your target. For example, a high roundhouse kick to your opponent's head without focus and power is as nothing compared to a roundhouse kick that is executed to your opponent's groin or knee with adequate focus and power.

G. Application of the roundhouse kick: method *b*

1. Suppose that your opponent comes at you with a weapon in his hand.
2. When you find a proper opening, suddenly deliver a strong front kick to your opponent's shin or knee to draw his attention to the lower part, and then execute the roundhouse kick to your opponent's temple, solar plexus, and/or groin.

1.

2. Deliver strong front kick to your opponent's shin to "freeze" him.

3. With a continuous movement of your other foot, deliver a high roundhouse kick to your opponent's temple.

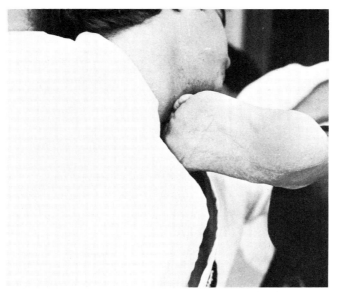

4. The roundhouse kick can also be delivered to your opponent's neck area.

Note: Normally, your opponent on the street will have no knowledge of karate and therefore will not expect your roundhouse kick. Your opponent will normally expect your attack to come straight from the front, and that's why your roundhouse kick can often be most effective in a self-defense situation.

Lesson 9

A. The side kick. Beginners find it much more difficult to learn the side kick than the front kick or the roundhouse kick. Since the human body is not structured by nature to perform the side kick, it must be properly trained and conditioned to perform it.

1. In preparation for the side kick, lift the kicking foot high.

2. Kick to the target straight sideward with the foot edge.

3. As you kick, make sure that your toes are curled up and your heel pushed outward so that your foot edge makes contact with the target.

4. It is important to have good balance in any kick, and the side kick is no exception. In order to create more stability and balance throughout the kick, your supporting foot should be flat on the floor (not on the ball) during and after kicking. In addition, the knee of your supporting leg should be slightly bent so that you can absorb the shock of kicking and pulling.

1. Look toward the direction in which you are about to kick.

2. Raise your kicking foot high.

3.

4.

5. The low side kick.

6. The middle side kick.

7. The high side kick.

8. The low side-thrust kick to your opponent's shin or knee.

9. The middle side kick applied to your opponent's floating rib area.

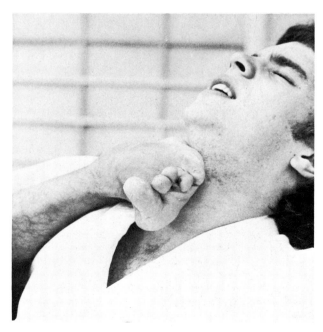

10. The high side kick applied to your opponent's throat.

B. Application of the side kick: method *a*
   1. As you receive an upper attack, step back
      slightly to adjust the distance between
      your opponent and you.
   2. Keep grabbing your opponent's attacking
      arm with your blocking arm.
   3. Deliver the side kick to your opponent's
      knee, ribs, throat, and/or face.

1. Block your opponent's attack.

2. Grab your opponent's attacking arm, and pull it slightly.

3. The side kick to your opponent's ribs.

4. The high side kick to your opponent's chin.

5.   6.

C. Application of the side kick: method *b*
1. As you confront an opponent with a weapon in his hand, watch the distance between you and your opponent.
2. When you find an opening, throw a strong side kick with a snapping motion to your opponent's shin area and follow it with another side kick to your opponent's throat or ribs.

1. You confront an opponent with a knife in his hand.

2. Measure the distance between you and your opponent closely and then suddenly execute a strong snapping side kick to your opponent's shin.

3. Make a final attack with a high side kick to your opponent's face.

4. The final attack can also be made to your opponent's midsection.

D. The crescent kick. The crescent kick can be used both defensively and offensively, although its more common use is as a blocking technique.

1. Raise your kicking foot high, and swing it inward with a semicircular motion.
2. When you practice alone, you can focus your crescent kick to the arm on the opposite side of your body, as shown in photos 1 and 2.

1.

2.

E. Application of the crescent kick: method *a*

1. As your opponent attempts the lunge attack, bend your upper body slightly backward to evade his punch.

2. Parry your opponent's attacking arm with the crescent kick.

3. With a continuous motion, get ready to execute the side kick.

4. Deliver the side kick to your opponent's lower ribs.

F. Application of the crescent kick: method *b*

1. Use the crescent kick in the same manner as in method *a*, but this time against an opponent with a knife.

2. Keep your eyes on your opponent's knife.

3. Close-up of the crescent kick to parry the arm with the weapon.

4. Use the crescent kick to parry the arm with the weapon.

5. With a continuous movement, execute a strong side kick to your opponent's ribs.

Lesson 10

A. Defense against an attack from behind: method *a*

1. Suppose that your opponent attacks you with two hands at the back of your neck. First, step back to move your right foot slightly closer to your opponent.
2. Then, step forward with your left foot, with the feeling of pulling away from your opponent.
3. While pulling away from your opponent, spin clockwise as you parry your opponent's right forearm with your right forearm.
4. Grab your opponent's right wrist immediately.

5. As you grab your opponent's right arm with both hands, pull your opponent forward to break his balance. (At this moment, you must step back slightly with your right foot.) Then deliver a strong front thrust kick to your opponent's midsection.
6. The front kick can be the final technique in a normal self-defense situation. If you want to execute a submission technique, apply pressure behind your opponent's right elbow with your left forearm while you place your opponent's right hand tightly high on your thigh.

Note: This final submission technique is an application of the technique you learned in Lesson 2C.

1. Your opponent chokes your neck from the back. (He can also just apply a hold on your shoulders from the back.)

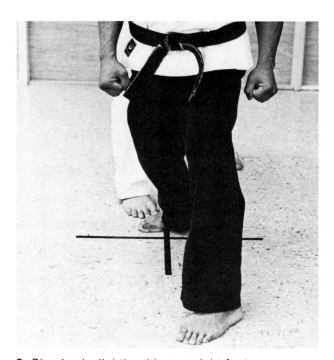

2. Step back slightly with your right foot.

3. Raise both arms high, and get ready to rotate your entire body.

4. As you step forward with your left foot with the feeling of pulling away from your opponent, spin your trunk and hip and try to parry your opponent's choking arms.

5. For the sake of maximum strength, you must twist your blocking arm too.

6. As you parry your opponent's arms, grab one of them with both hands and pull it forward to break his balance a little.

7. Execute a strong front kick to your opponent's midsection. Keep holding your opponent's arm.

8. Drop your left foot outside your opponent's right side, while your left arm is placed immediately behind your opponent's right elbow for pressure.

9. Turn your body around as you shift your weight to your right foot. Keep your opponent's arm high on your thigh tightly while you continuously press your opponent's right elbow.

10. The final submission is identical with the method described in Lesson 2C.

B. Defense against an attack from behind: method *b*

1. Your opponent attacks you from the back with his two hands.
2. Remove your opponent's attacking hands from the back of your neck in the same manner as in method *a*.
3. Thrust a left punch immediately to your opponent's face while you keep grabbing your opponent's right arm.
4. Bring your right foot outside your opponent's right foot.
5. Place your left foot between your opponent's feet while you bring your left arm around your opponent's neck.
6. Step back with your right foot as you complete your choking motion. At the final movement, your front foot (the left foot in this case) should be facing sideward for better leverage.
7. Make sure to keep the fist of your choking arm tightly clenched.

1.

2.

3.

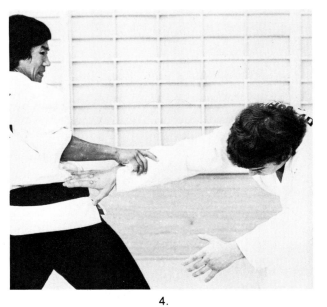

4.

5. A strong reverse punch to your opponent's temple area.

6.

7. As you choke, keep the fist of your choking arm clenched tightly and continue to grab your opponent's arm.

8. Your front foot (the left in this case) should be facing sideward for better leverage.

C. The back stance. The back stance is not an easy stance even for an advanced student. At the self-defense practice level, you do not really need this stance and you can easily replace it with the half-and-half stance.

1. Your feet must be in a straight line.
2. Your front foot points straight forward, and your back foot points sideward.
3. Over 70 percent of your weight rests on your back foot, and the remainder rests

on your front foot. Your back knee is fully bent, and your front knee is only very slightly bent.

4. Keep your back straight.

1. The front view.

2. The side view.

3.

4.

5. You can make a "minor" back stance by shortening the distance between your feet.

D. The double parrying block
1. Form an X with your arms in front of
your chest, with the palm side of your
fists toward your face.
2. As you twist your fists so that their palm
side faces outward, block off your opponent's attacking arms sideward.

1.

2.

3.

4.

E. Application of the double parrying block
   1. Your opponent comes at you and extends two arms either to choke you or to grab you from the front.
   2. By stepping back with either foot, and thus making a back stance (a regular one or a minor one), prepare to execute the double parrying block by crossing your arms with palm side of your fists toward you.
   3. Just before your opponent reaches your neck or shoulders, parry your opponent's arms.

1.

2.

3.

4. At the moment of blocking, utilize the back stance for more stability.

F. The front-knee kick. The front-knee kick can be executed from either the front stance position or the natural stance position.

1. Suppose you practice it now from the front stance position.

2. Bring the back foot forward and upward as shown. The toes of the kicking leg should be curled at the moment the front–knee kick is executed.

3. Let's also practice the front–knee kick from the natural stance.

1.

2.

3.

4.

G. Application of the front-knee kick
    1. By applying the double parrying block against your opponent's two-arms attack from the front, you are in position to deliver the front knee kick to your opponent's solar plexus or groin, and if you grab the back of your opponent's neck, you can bring him down to deliver the front knee-kick to his face.
    2. After you block your opponent's attack with the back stance or minor front stance, prepare for the knife hand attack.
    3. Execute the double knife hand attack from both sides up and down diagonally to the sides of your opponent's neck.
    4. Grab the back of your opponent's neck immediately with both hands.
    5. Execute the front-knee kick as you pull your opponent's head down and forward.

1.

2.

3.

4.

5.

6. The final attack with the front knee kick to your opponent's midsection (a kick to the solar plexus is most effective).

7. The front knee kick to your opponent's groin.

8. The front knee kick to your opponent's face.

H. The roundhouse knee kick
1. As with the regular roundhouse kick with the foot, in order to execute the roundhouse knee kick you bring your knee high into the ready position.
2. Propel your entire body as you turn your supporting foot 90 degrees, and simultaneously deliver the roundhouse knee kick to the target.

1. The ready position for the roundhouse knee kick.

2. At the moment you execute the roundhouse knee kick, your supporting foot should turn about 90 degrees for greater stability and power.

3. Let's look at the roundhouse knee kick from another angle.

4.

I. Application of the roundhouse knee kick
    1. Block your opponent's upper attack, and grab his attacking arm immediately with your blocking arm.
    2. As you step outside your opponent's right foot with your left foot (if your opponent attempts the right upper attack as illustrated here), keep grabbing your opponent's attacking arm.
    3. Bring your kicking leg high to prepare for the roundhouse knee kick.
    4. Execute the roundhouse knee kick to your opponent's solar plexus area.

1.

2.

3.

4.

5. The roundhouse knee kick can also be executed against your opponent's groin.

6. The roundhouse knee kick against your opponent's face.

7. The flying-roundhouse knee kick to your opponent's temple. (The flying-roundhouse knee kick is not for beginners. Moreover, it is not a practical technique in actual self-defense.)

Lesson 11

A. Defense against the one-arm choke from the back

1. Your opponent attacks you from behind and chokes you with his right arm. (Needless to say, you must also practice this defense against a left arm attack.)
2. Pull your chin down immediately, hold your opponent's choking arm with your right hand, and bring your right foot inside your opponent's right foot.
3. As you pull your left foot back to bring it closer to your opponent and inside your opponent's left foot, execute the left back elbow strike to weaken your opponent.
4. Bend both knees and hold your opponent's inside your left knee, and at the same time keep a tight hold on your opponent's right arm with your right hand.
5. Push your knees upward as you pull your right arm down, and at the same time push upward at the inside of your opponent's left knee.
6. To complete the whole throwing movement, pull your opponent's right arm until his body falls to the ground. The springing knee action, together with the pulling motion of the right arm is very important in this technique.

Follow photos 1 to 10 step by step carefully.

1.

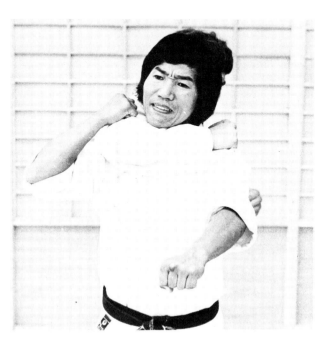

2. Grab your opponent's choking arm, and prepare your left arm for the back elbow strike.

3. The moment of the back elbow strike.

4. Make sure that your right foot is inside your opponent's right foot.

5. Step back with your left foot until it is inside your opponent's left foot.

6. Make sure that your knees are bent sufficiently and that your left hand holds your opponent's inside left knee.

7. With a strong springing action of both knees, together with a pulling motion of your right hand and an upward pushing motion of your left hand, throw your opponent over your shoulder.

8. Of course, when you practice with your partner, extreme caution is required for safety in throwing and in being thrown. Let's study carefully the basic falling method in Chapter 3.

9.

10.

Let's look at this technique from another angle.

11.

12.

13.

14.

B. The one-arm shoulder throw against an upper attack

1. Block your opponent's upper attack (the open block).
2. Grab your opponent's attacking arm quickly with your blocking arm.
3. You may or may not execute the upper reverse punch to your opponent's face, solar plexus, or groin.
4. Keep grabbing your opponent's attacking arm with your blocking arm (your left arm in this case), and bring your right foot inside your opponent's right foot. At this moment, also grab your opponent's right upper arm with the upper part of your right arm by pushing against your opponent's right armpit.

5. Push your back against your opponent's front by pulling back your left foot to the inside of your opponent's left foot, and make sure that you push your hip out toward your right. Bend the knees enough so that you can spring up at the moment you throw your opponent.
6. In throwing your opponent, you must synchronize three forces: the force that pulls down your opponent's right arm, the springing motion of both your knees, and the twisting motion of your hip.

Follow photos 1 to 6 slowly and carefully. Again, when you practice with your partner, you must execute 100 percent control so that you do not hurt your partner, and vice versa.

1.

2. This freezing technique can be applied against your opponent's face or groin.

3. Bring your right foot inside your opponent's right foot.

4. As you bring your left foot all the way back to inside your opponent's left knee, bend both your knees fully to prepare for a springing action.

5.

6.

C. The side-elbow strike to finish with a take-down on knee

1. Block your opponent's right middle attack with your right outside-inside block by stepping back with your left foot into the half-and-half stance.
2. Grab your opponent's attacking arm (the right arm in this case) with your left hand.
3. Deliver the right side-elbow strike by making the straddle stance, and keep holding your opponent's right hand.
4. After executing the right side-elbow strike, bend your right knee to the ground and press your right forearm against your opponent's inside right knee.
5. Hold the back of your opponent's ankle with your left hand.
6. Throw your opponent by two actions: pushing the inside of his knee and pulling his ankle with your left hand.
7. If necessary, complete the throw with a final attack by punching to your opponent's groin.

1. The outside-inside block.

2. Grab your opponent's attacking arm immediately, and prepare for the side-elbow attack.

3. Keep holding your opponent's arm as you execute the side-elbow attack.

4. After you "freeze" your opponent with the side-elbow attack, place your right forearm against your opponent's right inner knee while your other hand holds your opponent's ankle.

5. By synchronizing the pushing force against your opponent's inner knee and the pulling force on your opponent's ankle, throw your opponent to the ground.

6. If necessary, you may punch your opponent's groin.

D. Defense against a full-nelson hold

1. First attack your opponent's eyes, reaching back to temporarily weaken him so that you can bend forward a little. This can also be accomplished by kicking your opponent's instep or shin.

2. As soon as you bend forward a little, move your right foot outside your opponent's right foot and hold your opponent's right wrist with your right hand.

3. Bring your left foot around behind your opponent's right foot.

4. Push the back of your opponent's right knee with the front of your left knee, and make one strong counterclockwise shaking motion with your hip and trunk, still holding your opponent's right arm tightly.

5. As your opponent falls to the ground, turn around to face him immediately, and don't let your opponent's right arm go off your hand. (By this time, you should be holding your opponent's right arm with both hands.)

6. You may vary your final attack. In the technique shown in photo 7, for example, you push your opponent's right temple area with your left knee while you press your opponent's right arm against your right thigh with a dislocating motion.

1. Your opponent grabs you from the back with the full-nelson hold.

2. If necessary, deliver an attack to your opponent's eyes.

3. Bring your body forward as you move your right foot next to your opponent's right foot.

4. Bring your left leg behind your opponent's right leg.

5. With a strong shaking motion of your hip and trunk, throw your opponent to your back.

6. Spin back immediately to see your opponent on the ground.

7. You may vary your final attack. For example, you may attack your opponent on the ground by pushing his temple with your left knee while you press his right arm against your right leg.

8. Your final attack may also be a stamping kick to the side of your opponent's neck.

9. At the moment of takedown, you may lift your opponent up and backward instead of just shaking and throwing him.

10. You must keep holding your opponent's arm after the throw.

E. The hip throw against an upper attack: method *a*

1. Your opponent lunges in with the right upper punch, which you evade to his inside by immediately grabbing his left hand to stop his second attack.

2. Grab around your opponent's hip with your left arm, and bring your foot inside your opponent's left foot.

3. Bring back your right foot inside your opponent's right foot, and bend both your knees fully so that you are ready for a springing motion.

4. Push your hip out slightly to your left so that your opponent cannot easily escape by slipping out from your left side.

5. In order to throw your opponent, you must synchronize three forces: the pulling motion of your right arm, the springing up action of both your knees, and the twisting motion of your hip. This maneuver is more effective if you try to keep your back as straight as possible at the moment you bend your knees (just before the springing motion).

1.

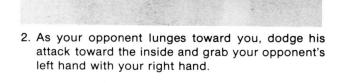

2. As your opponent lunges toward you, dodge his attack toward the inside and grab your opponent's left hand with your right hand.

3. As you place your left arm around your opponent's waist, bring your left foot directly inside your opponent's left foot. Keep holding your opponent's left hand.

4. Pull down your opponent's left arm as you bring your right foot inside your opponent's right foot. Throw your hip toward your left to ensure that your opponent does not slip off.

5. Throw your opponent by synchronizing three forces: the springing action of your knees, the upward pull of your hips, and the downward pull of your right arm.

6. In practice with your partner, it is not necessary for the two of you to throw each other too hard. When you throw your partner, it is important to keep a tight hold around his waist area.

F. The hip throw against an upper attack: method *b*

1. Block your opponent's right upper lunge attack with the left upper block by stepping back with your right foot and assuming the half-and-half stance.

2. Grab your opponent's right wrist with your left hand, and deliver the right reverse punch to your opponent's face (below the nose).

3. Keep holding your opponent's right arm, and bring your right foot inside your opponent's right foot as you hold your right arm around your opponent's waist.

4. Step back with your left foot to bring it inside your opponent's left foot, and push your right hip out.

5. Bend both your knees fully in order to be ready for the springing action.

6. As in method *a*, the pull of your left arm, the spring of both your knees, and the twisting of your hip must be well synchronized with one another and with the right arm around your opponent's waist.

1. Against your opponent's right upper lunge attack, step back with your right foot and execute the left upper block (the open block).

2. Bring your right foot inside your opponent's right foot, and at the same time bring your right arm around your opponent's waist. Keep holding your opponent's original attacking arm (the right arm in this case).

3. Pull down your opponent's right arm strongly, and throw your hip toward your right to prevent your opponent's body from slipping off your hip. Keep your right arm tightly around your opponent's waist. Bend your knees enough to be able to spring up.

4. Throw your opponent by synchronizing the springing action of your knees, the motion of your hip with your right arm, and the pull of your left arm.

5.

6.

Lesson 12

A. Defense from the ground: method *a*

1. You are on the ground, and your opponent is on his/her feet, ready to attack you.
2. At the moment you find an opportunity, kick your opponent's groin or shin to throw your opponent off guard, and then make a scissors against either of your opponent's legs.
3. Pushing one foot and pulling the other against your opponent's leg, throw him/her to the ground.

1. As your opponent comes close to you when you are on the ground, execute a strong kick to his shin or groin in order to "freeze" him.

2. Bring one of your feet inside your opponent's knee and the other foot behind your opponent's ankle.

3. By pulling your opponent's ankle from behind while you push your opponent's knee from inside, you throw him to his back.

4. After you throw your opponent, get to your feet immediately. (Practice both sides.)

B. Defense from the ground: method *b*
1. You are on the ground, and your opponent comes at you with both hands extended to grab you.
2. Grab both of your opponent's arms, and place one of your feet against his abdominal area.
3. Utilizing your opponent's momentum, push his abdomen with your foot and at the same time strongly pull both of his arms over your face.
4. With this technique, as with the other self-defense techniques explained in this book, after you acquire a basic knowledge of the technique, the most important thing that you must do is to perfect your timing and coordination of the entire technique. You can accomplish this by repeated practice.

1. If your opponent comes at you when you are on the ground, take the position of defense as shown here.

2. As your opponent is about to grab your neck, catch both of his arms and place one of your feet on his stomach area.

3. To throw your opponent over your body, synchronize three forces: the pulling force of both your arms, the pushing force of one of your feet, and your opponent's momentum.

4. Get to your feet immediately after you throw your opponent.

C. Defense from the ground: method *c*

1. As your opponent attempts to grab your collar by extending both arms, grab one of them quickly and twist the wrist inward.

2. Keep applying pressure to twist your opponent's wrist inward, and turn around and get up to force your opponent to submit.

1. You are on the ground, and your opponent is about to attack you.

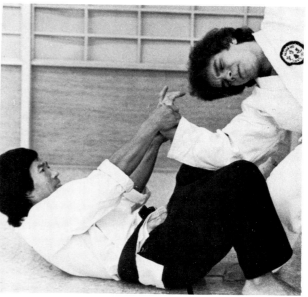

2. As soon as your opponent extends his arms to attack you, immediately grab one of his hands to execute a wristlock.

3. In order to execute the wristlock effectively, push your opponent's hand from its back toward its inside.

4. As you make your wrist-bend technique effective, get up immediately and force your opponent's submission.

D. Defense from the ground: method *d*
   1. Grab one of your opponent's arms quickly, and apply pressure behind it.
   2. By getting up quickly and still holding your opponent's arm and applying pressure behind the elbow, force your opponent to submit.

1.

2. As your opponent extends his hands to attack you, grab one of them immediately and then kick his stomach in order to "freeze" him.

3. Turn your body to get up, and at the same time apply pressure to the arm that you just grabbed. Your pressure should be applied directly to the back of your opponent's elbow.

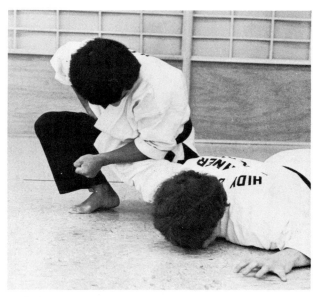

4. Swing your body hard and fast to get up and finish the submission. (This technique is a little difficult to master initially, and as with any other technique it takes patience and effort to really "know" it.)

E. Defense against a gunpoint: method *a*
1. As your opponent points a gun at the back of your neck, spin quickly to parry the hand in which your opponent is holding the gun.
2. Immediately, execute the roundhouse knee kick to your opponent's groin or solar plexus.
3. Force your opponent to submit by applying pressure to the back of his/her elbow.

1. If you feel a gunpoint at the back of your neck, raise both your hands to show that you have no intention of resisting the threat.

2. Suddenly and quickly spin and parry the hand with the gun.

3. Execute the roundhouse knee kick to your opponent's midsection while continuing to hold the hand with the gun.

4. The final submission.

Let's look at this technique from another angle.

5.

6.

7.

8.

Note: Obviously, any self-defense technique against a gun threat is very serious. It requires a great deal of mental and physical strength together with speed of the technique. It is best not to react against a gun, therefore, unless you are 100 percent sure of the situation. However, practice of such technique is important in the sense that it teaches us to become more alert mentally and more coordinated physically.

F. Defense against a gunpoint: method *b*

1. As your opponent points a gun at your chest area, raise your hands to show that you have no intention of resisting the threat.

2. Suddenly and quickly, drop both arms, using one of them to parry the hand in which your opponent is holding the gun and the other to attack your opponent's face with a back-fist strike or a palm-heel strike.

3. With a continuous movement, twist your opponent's arm by bending its elbow with both your arms.

4. Your final submission technique is to push back your opponent's arm by applying continuous pressure to the wrist.

1.

2. As you parry the hand in which your opponent is holding a gun, deliver a strong back-fist thrust to your opponent's face.

3. The front-knee kick can also be applied to "freeze" your opponent before you take him down for the final submission.

4.

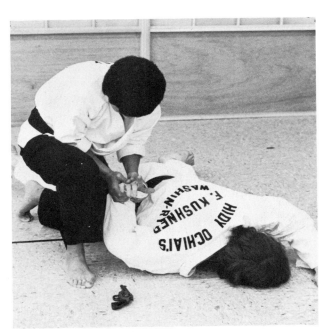

5. The final submission.

6. Of course, there are many different ways in which you can deal with this situation. Here is another.

7. Drop both your hands as you make an X form and parry the hand with the gun to either side.

8. With a continuous motion, grab the hand in which your opponent is holding the gun. Here you can apply such freezing techniques as the back-fist strike to the opponent's temple or the front-knee kick. The final submission can be the same as that shown in photos 4 and 5.

3

Basic falling techniques

As a part of self-defense knowledge, it is essential to learn the basic falling methods. Falling (which is called *u-ke-mi* in Japanese) can be a highly refined art in itself, but for our purposes we concentrate on only the very basic falling techniques.

A. The back fall. In the *back fall*, the most important thing to keep in mind is not to hit your head. You can avoid having the back of your head hit the ground by pulling your chin tightly downward.

1. Take the squatting position on the balls of your feet. Keep your arms crossed in front of your chest.

183

2. Fall gently on your hip as you raise both your arms high to absorb the impact of the fall.

3. As you fall from your hip to your back, you are ready to absorb the impact of the fall.

4. Hit the floor hard with both your arms flat and straight as you keep your eyes on your stomach (in other words, pull your chin tightly downward). Your whole body should be rather relaxed; you should keep the feeling of making your body small.

Let us look at the back fall from another view.

5.

6.

7.

8.

B. The front fall. In the *front fall,* you must remember that it is of the utmost importance to protect your face, and so at the moment of falling, it is best to look slightly sideward. It is also essential to protect your knees and to make sure that they do not hit the ground.

1. Sit on your knees.

2. Raise both arms halfway.

3. As you fall forward, slam the floor with both arms as far up as the elbows. Lift your knees from the ground at the moment you take the fall.

Let's look at the front fall from another angle.

4.

5.

6. At the moment of falling it is a good idea to look sideward in order to protect your face.

C. The side fall. In the *side fall*, the most important thing to keep in mind is to receive the whole impact of the fall on one side only (on either arm). In other words, if you are taking the side fall with your right arm, your weight and the impact of the fall should be fully received by the right arm only.

Practice the falling techniques slowly and gently in the beginning.

1. From the natural stance.

2. Raise one foot high as the arm on the same side comes up high.

3. Bend the knee of your supporting leg gently, and fall sideward.

4. Receive the impact of the fall with one arm (the left arm in this case).

Let's practice the side fall with the other arm.

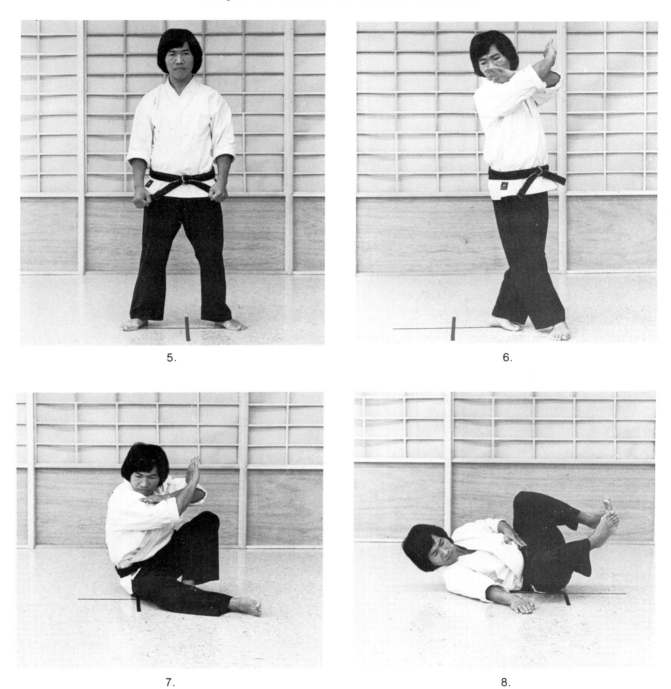

5.

6.

7.

8.

Note: As with the back fall, the arm that hits the ground should be open approximately 45 degrees from your body—not too wide and not too narrow.

Main pressure points and how to attack them

Here we concentrate only on those points that we are most likely to recognize readily and to use under normal circumstances.

A. The skull

By hammer fist. (You can also attack the skull with the dropping-elbow strike when your opponent tries to tackle you.)

B. The base of the skull

By the dropping-elbow strike. (You can also punch the base of the skull if your opponent turns his back to you.)

C. The temple

1. By roundhouse kick.

2. By roundhouse back-fist strike.

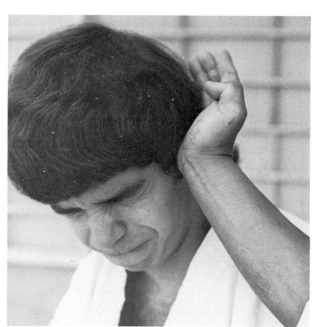

3. By knife-hand strike.

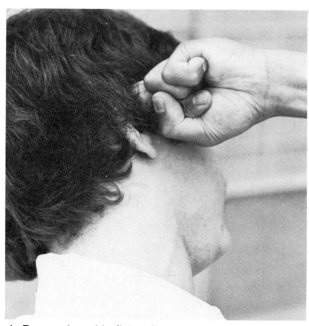

4. By one-knuckle fist strike.

D. The bridge of the nose

1. By punch.

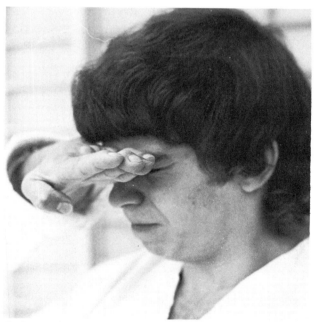

2. By knife-hand strike.

3. By front-knee kick.

E. The base of the nose

1. By punch.

2. By palm-heel strike.

3. By back kick with heel.

4. By side kick

F. The jaw

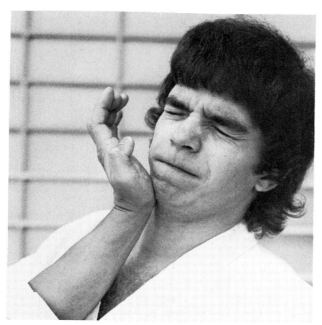

1. By palm-heel strike.

2. By punch.

3. By upper-elbow and side-elbow strikes.

4. By roundhouse kick.

G. The chin

1. By upper-elbow strike.

2. By palm-heel strike.

3. By front kick. (A side kick to the chin can also be effective.)

H. The Adam's apple

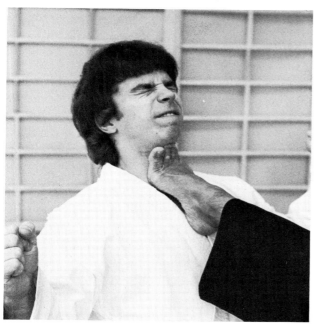

1. By front kick.

2. By punch.

3. By back-heel kick.

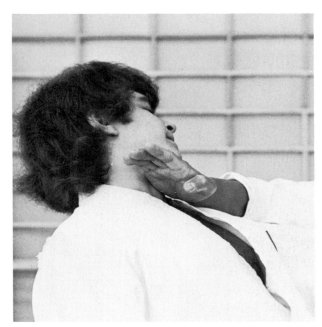

4. By knife hand.

5. By side kick.

I. The side of the neck

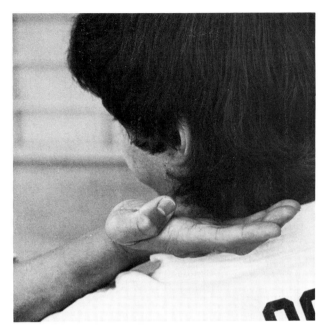

1. By knife hand (a).

2. By knife hand (b).

J. The solar plexus

1. By front-heel kick. (a front kick with the ball of the foot is also good).

2. By roundhouse kick.

3. By punch. (A one-knuckle fist to the solar plexus is also effective.)

4. By back-elbow strike.

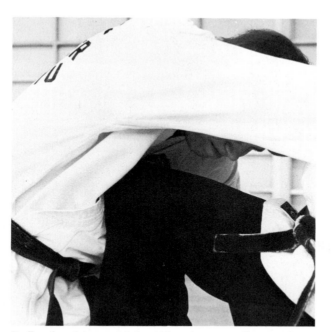

5. By front-knee kick. (Also by roundhouse knee kick.)

K. The floating ribs

1. By roundhouse kick. (Other kicking techniques, such as the side kick and the front kick, can also be applied here.)

2. By punch.

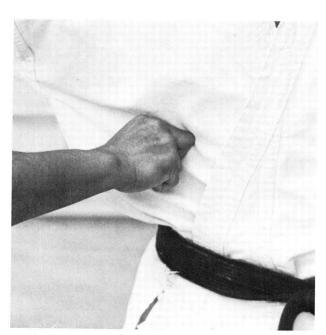

3. By one-knuckle fist strike.

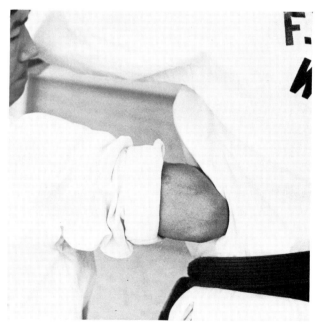

4. By front-elbow strike.

L. The abdomen

1. By front kick.

2. By side kick.

3. By punch.

4. By back kick with heel.

M. The groin

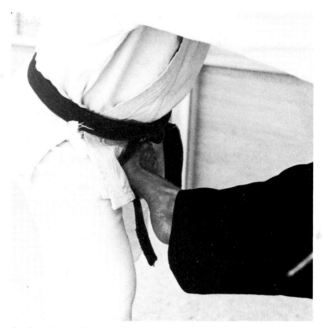

1. By front-knee kick. (Or by roundhouse knee kick.)

2. By front kick.

3. By back kick with heel. (In certain situations the punch and the palm-heel strike can be applied effectively here.)

N. The inner thigh

1. By front kick.

2. By roundhouse kick. (Also by palm-heel strike, punch, back kick, etc.)

O. The knee

1. By front kick.

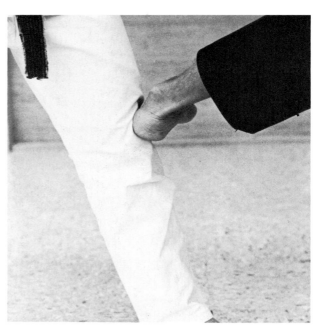

2. By side kick.

3. Inside knee can be attacked by knife-hand strike.

4. Inside knee can be attacked by front-elbow strike.

P. The shin

1. By side kick.

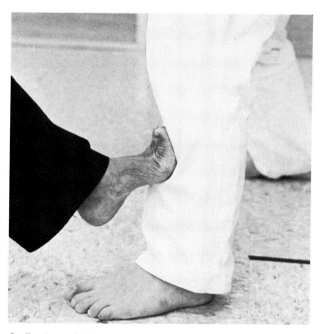

2. By front kick.

3. By back-heel kick.

Q. The instep

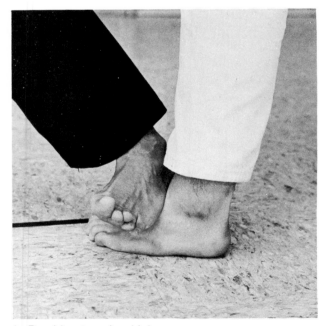

1. By side-stamping kick.

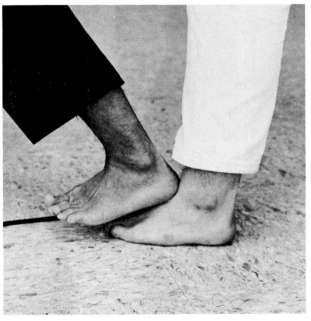

2. By back-stamping kick with the heel. (Also by front-stamping kick.)

R. Other important but less apparent pressure points
1. The windpipe.
2. The base of the neck.
3. The collarbone (clavicle).
4. The armpit.
5. The upper arm (biceps and triceps).
6. The upper back.
7. The center of the back.
8. The kidney.
9. The coccyx.
10. The calf.
11. The Achilles' tendon, etc.

Note: The reason for the importance of pressure points is the fact that you can increase and ensure the effectiveness of your defensive techniques by utilizing your opponent's pressure points, whenever you can. For example, your punch as a counter-attack may be more effective if it is directed to your opponent's solar plexus or to the base of the nose rather than your opponent's chest area. In other words, you can economize your energy in executing the techniques. On the other hand, if you practice with a partner, you should be extremely careful in executing your techniques by controlling 100 percent so that you do not hurt your partner, even by mistake, when you are dealing with pressure points.

Index